Sampling
Life

100 Ways to Find Joy
in Unemployment

RAINA RUSNAK

Illustrations: Sage Ferrari

If you are struggling with depression or other mental health issues, please seek the guidance and care of a trained professional. This book is not intended to be a substitute for customized personal care.

The reader assumes all risks, responsibilities, and liabilities associated with any activities inspired by the suggestions in this book. For activities where alcohol is an option, please drink responsibly.

ISBN: 979-8-9916306-1-0 (Ebook)
ISBN: 979-8-9916306-0-3 (Paperback)
ISBN: 979-8-9916306-2-7 (Hardcover)

Imprint: 750 Research

For Sage, who helps me stay grounded.

And whether or not it is clear to you, no doubt the universe is unfolding as it should.

— *Max Ehrmann, "Desiderata"*

TABLE OF CONTENTS

BE ACTIVE 123

WHAT NOW?

Welcome to unemployment. Let's be real: the situation sucks. I've been there.

For several years, I had my dream job leading consumer insights for a Fortune 500 company. Understanding customer needs, pain points, and desires through the pandemic and guiding the business to make strategic decisions as the voice of the customer was nothing short of a thrill. Back-to-back meetings filled every typical business minute, followed by hours of working in the evening to deliver on the promises made in those nonstop meetings. Then, suddenly, inflationary pressures hit. A restructure and significant layoffs found my role with the company gone, like a plug pulled from a drain.

Shortly following my layoff notice, I found an article from a man who had returned to work after his own job search. He counseled that this time is temporary and urged other job seekers to stay strong. I subsequently read about others who used their time off to travel, bolster their education, and immerse themselves in a variety of other stimulating activities. Admittedly, at first I rolled my eyes and thought, "Well, bully for you." But once I flipped a mental switch, I felt inspired to seize the opportunity in front of me. I was burned out and desperately in need of a reset. The year that followed replenished and restored my depleted emotional state.

I chaperoned school field trips, volunteered with three different organizations, wrote a book, worked out regularly at the boxing gym, and started my own consulting business. I presented at my first LinkedIn Live event, attended two conferences, and sought a new professional certification.

I tackled home projects: patched walls, repaired the deck, replaced rotting boards around my patio, cleaned out closets, organized the basement, and donated carloads of items to charity.

I applied to be a ball girl in the U.S. Open and submitted a video to be a contestant on a reality show. Neither of those panned out, but the anticipation of potentially being called energized me.

I attended my first polo match, learned the "Thriller" dance, tried my hand at disc golf, and at the instruction of middle schoolers played my first game of gaga ball. I ate my way through town on a walking doughnut tour, burned off those calories rock climbing, and attended a college reunion.

I read dozens of books. *Dozens.* I hadn't read a single book in almost five years. Not because I didn't want to, but because I was too exhausted after a long day of work. Gosh, it felt good to be back in that world.

I reconnected with former colleagues I hadn't seen in years, spent quality time with family and friends, and even made new friends, a nice yield to hundreds of networking video calls.

Winter afforded the opportunity for skiing out West. In spring, I became a tourist in my own town, soaking in the beauty of Washington, DC's cherry blossom trees. Summer found me singing off-key from my blanket on the grass at an outdoor performance of one of my favorite bands from college. In autumn, I sought formal education in wine.

The year of unemployment underscored for me the value of self-care, being present, reconnecting with people, trying new things, staying active, learning, and actually seeing the world around me. I met hundreds of people, made new friends, learned new skills, traveled on a budget, and pushed myself outside of my comfort zone. While I would have opted for this chapter in my life to close as soon as possible, the gifts it offered were necessary for my mental health and sent me on an important journey of self-discovery.

This is where you might be rolling your own eyes, and I get it. The reality is that no matter what cool adventures you may embark on while out of work, you will also spend countless hours applying to jobs, customizing resumes, writing cover letters, and networking like it's a full-time job. And yes, some companies will lead you on and demand weeks of your time before ghosting you like a bad date. Have I mentioned this sucks?

And then there is the stress, uncertainty, and financial obligations, the worry about the future. This experience may very well be the rollercoaster you never wanted to ride. Highs and lows all on the same day. Making it through this will take grit, determination, fortitude, and a support network. That's where this book comes in. The inspiration for it began during a networking video call when a peer noted that my encouragement, outlook, and suggestions helped them overcome significant depression after losing their job. Many others have since shared similar sentiments.

As a researcher by trade, I suppose it was fitting for me to conduct qualitative interviews with others along the same journey, asking such questions as, "What kept you positive during your time of unemployment?" The answer that came from one baby boomer female, in particular, surprised me. "I got my motorcycle license ... and a leather jacket." This shocked me not because of the person's age or gender, but because she is my mother. And I had absolutely no idea she had her motorcycle license!

This book combines my own experiences with what has kept others grounded and positive during tough times. It is the collective voice of people who have walked a mile in your shoes.

My aim is to guide you in spending time enjoying your period of unemployment. That's right. Give yourself permission to appreciate and even relish it.

Picture this: Future You has landed a new role and looks back at Current You. Will Future You regret squandering this time away worrying, or will you remember appreciating and making the most of this opportunity?

Your journey will undoubtedly look different from mine and from those alongside you. Let the suggestions in this book inspire you to experience what makes you feel joyful and stay positive. Prioritize what is most important for you to accomplish while you are time-rich.

May you enjoy the benefits of stretching your mind, deepening connections, and exploring new frontiers. Appreciate the experiences you have in the moment because this time, as that LinkedIn author so thoughtfully articulated, is truly temporary.

Now, let's find your motorcycle license/leather jacket equivalent and go after it.

HOW TO USE THIS BOOK

The following pages offer inspiration and space for reflection.

There's no right way to use them. Skip around. Select an activity that suits your mood on that particular day and feel free to modify based on your needs and circumstances. Track your progress in the table of contents. Use different colored pens if that inspires you.

Take the ideas that work for you; shed the rest. But do try to keep an open mind. You might surprise yourself with how much you grow by staying open. Perhaps you're not normally the type to get on a rock wall. With this road map, you may just unleash your inner Alex Honnold.

Each activity or mission will offer space for notes or reflections, sometimes with prompts specific to the task. Use these sections to jot down future plans, celebrate your progress, or explore your own introspection.

Feel free to undertake multiple missions per day—make homemade ice cream and enjoy the fruits of your labor outside on a blanket—two items checked. Some of these adventures take a few minutes, while others require multiple days or even weeks.

Remember this is *your* workbook to use in whatever way works best for you. Try a different activity each day, commit to making measurable daily progress on larger goals, or just come here when you need a bit of inspiration. Allow yourself to go back and repeat suggestions.

Feel free to inspire others walking this same road. If you feel comfortable, share your progress on social media with #samplinglife. Forming a supportive community makes this journey more memorable and enjoyable.

Once you have landed in a new role, flip back through the pages to reflect on how positively you spent your transition time. And with the time in between accepting an offer and starting the new role, see how many more pursuits you can accomplish.

As a starting point, consider what you have always wanted to do then sketch out a plan that brings it to life. Now, grab your favorite colored pen or pencil and turn the page—let the adventure begin!

EXPAND YOUR PALATE

Let's start by nourishing your body and brain. Our working selves may seldom have had time to prepare meals, sometimes leaning heavily into takeout as a solution. Now, we can mindfully take the time to explore and create what tastes great to us, lifts us. While not every mission in this section is about cooking, each idea will challenge you to expand your tastes, try new things, and reap the inspiration that flows from the different experiences.

1. CRAFT A BREAKFAST BURRITO

Years ago, a colleague and friend commented on how when you're unemployed, you have the time to make a breakfast burrito if you want one. My typical breakfast at that time generally involved a quick bowl of cereal or frozen waffles heated in the toaster oven. This concept of slowing down and savoring the morning resonated with me. When I found myself unemployed, I decided to give it a try. What a rewarding experience!

I begin here because the simple act of making a breakfast burrito is achievable in a short amount of time and is a delicious way to kick off your day and your journey. In building a burrito, start small or go big. The simplicity or complexity of the creation hinges on your own customized desires. And, when you're finished with this mission, you can savor the outcome of your labor.

Allow a breakfast burrito to symbolize for you what it did for me—a celebration of an achievement and promise of what's to come.

To elevate this dish, lightly crisp the filled burrito in one tablespoon of oil or butter. The finished product will hold together with better consistency and reward you with enhanced taste. For extra heat, add a dash of hot sauce to your final creation.

HERE IS MY GO-TO BREAKFAST BURRITO RECIPE FOR ONE:

- 1 large russet potato peeled and diced
- 2 eggs
- A splash of milk
- (optional) 1/2 orange pepper or yellow pepper, diced
- (optional) 1/2 small yellow onion, diced
- 1/8 cup cheddar cheese
- 1 10-inch soft flour tortilla shell
- 2 Tbsps. vegetable oil
- Hot sauce to taste
- Salt and pepper to taste

1. In a pan over medium heat, cook diced potatoes in 1 tablespoon of vegetable oil, adding kosher salt to taste, for about 20 minutes or until a touch crisp. Stir occasionally.
2. If cooking with onion and pepper, add to the mixture. Cook for another 10 minutes.
3. Whisk eggs with a splash of milk, salt, and pepper to taste. Add the egg mixture when the potato and pepper are to your liking. Stir constantly until eggs are fully cooked.

4. Fill tortillas with the potato and egg mixture, sprinkle in cheese, and wrap it up.

5. Using the same pan, add another tablespoon of vegetable oil and lightly crisp the two burritos side by side on medium heat. Start this process by placing the opening side down. Flip the first time after the shell feels like it's firming up and will hold together, about 2 minutes. Crisp the remaining side for another 90 seconds or until desired consistency.

6. For extra fun, I like to mix ranch salad dressing with hot sauce and use as a dip for my burrito.

DATE COMPLETED:

_____

ADD YOUR NOTES ON THE FILLING HERE:

_____

_____

_____

_____

_____

_____

_____

_____

_____

_____

_____

_____

_____

_____

2. PREPARE A NEW DISH

This is your chance to satisfy a craving and express creativity. What dish have you been inspired to make, but never quite had the motivation to execute? Is it the family lasagna that's been calling to you? Or a crab cake recipe you haven't mustered enough motivation to start? Perhaps you're craving a homemade stew or simply feel inspired to experiment with a more exotic vegetable than your usual zucchini.

Spend a moment reflecting on what you have wanted to make, but have not had the time or energy to take on. Select a recipe for a main meal that serves your full household.

Prepare a list of what you need, go shopping, and get to work crafting a delicious masterpiece.

If you're seeking additional inspiration, here is an easy recipe that my family requests for dinner regularly.

SIMPLE VEGETARIAN BLACK BEAN CHILI

- 2 15 oz cans black beans, drained and rinsed
- 1 bunch scallions, chopped (white and green parts)
- 1 16 oz jar of mild salsa

- 1 10 oz bag of frozen super sweet corn
- 1 bunch of cilantro, chopped
- Cooked rice (optional)
- Shredded cheddar cheese (optional)

The flavor from this recipe hinges on the salsa, so choose that selection thoughtfully.

1. Combine black beans, scallions, and salsa in saucepan. Cover and cook over medium heat for 10 minutes, stirring occasionally.

2. Prepare the frozen corn per instructions on the packaging.

3. Stir in corn, cilantro, and salt to taste. Cook until heated through, stirring occasionally.

4. Serve hot topped with shredded cheddar cheese over a bed of rice, if desired.

5. TIP: Double the recipe and freeze half for later. It reheats nicely.

DATE COMPLETED:

_____

DISH PREPARED:

_____

NOTES:

_____

_____

_____

_____

_____

_____

_____

_____

_____

_____

3. MAKE HOMEMADE ICE CREAM OR SORBET

If you have an ice cream maker gathering dust on the top shelf of your cabinet, climb that step stool and bring it down. If you don't have one, no worries: Ice cream or sorbet can be made in at least four other ways. Hard to believe, so I'll outline what I've learned below.

#1. PLASTIC BAG METHOD

I have personally tried this method several times with great success and delight.

1. Prepare your ice cream mixture then add to a quart size resealable bag, removing as much air as possible.

2. Place inside a gallon size bag. Fill with 3.5 cups of crushed ice and 3.5 tablespoons of salt.

3. Remove as much air as possible from the gallon bag and seal.

4. Shake vigorously and squeeze the bag regularly to ensure that the ice does its job with the ice cream mixture.

Our Girl Scout Troop has fun with this by squeezing the bags in their underarms, calling it armpit ice cream. However you decide to squeeze the bag, with your underarms or hands, do this for about 7 minutes or until the ice cream is frozen.

#2. ELECTRIC MIXER METHOD

1. Whip two cups of heavy whipping cream with an electric mixer until stiff peaks form (about 5 minutes).
2. Slowly add a chilled can of sweetened condensed milk.
3. Combine any mix-ins or other flavors.
4. Seal in an airtight, freezer safe container. Freeze 4-6 hours or until firm.

#3. FOOD PROCESSOR METHOD

1. Prepare the ice cream mixture according to your recipe. When the instructions call for the ice cream maker, pour into a resealable bag and remove all air.
2. Freeze until solid.
3. Break into pieces then food process until smooth.
4. Fold in any mix-ins.
5. Seal and freeze the final product.

#4. STIRRING METHOD

1. Prepare the ice cream mixture according to your recipe. When time for the ice cream maker, pour into a freezable baking dish.
2. Every 30 minutes for approximately 3 hours, stir the mixture and return to freezer.
3. After three hours, freeze final product.

Research a recipe for your favorite flavor and make an afternoon of it. Perhaps a simple chocolate sounds divine. Or maybe venture out with a peanut butter, banana, or caramel — or all three in one.

Dairy free? Consider a sorbet. Perhaps lemon or raspberry.

Feeling like a challenge? Commit to making homemade ice cream without a maker via four different methods. Then recruit friends or family to taste test and offer their perspective on which method yielded the tastiest results.

Here's one of my go-to recipes for a base.

HOMEMADE RASPBERRY ICE CREAM

- 3 large egg yolks
- ¾ cup sugar
- ½ cup water
- 1 pound of red raspberries
- ¼ tsp salt (I put in between ¼ and ½ tsp depending on my mood)
- 1 tablespoon lemon juice
- 2 cups half-and-half

1. Place the yolks in a food processor. Set aside.
2. Combine the sugar and water in a saucepan over low heat. Stir until the sugar dissolves to make a simple syrup.
3. Once the simple syrup is clear, turn the heat to high and bring to a boil. Boil for 3 minutes without stirring.
4. Begin running the food processor housing your egg yolks. Slowly pour the hot syrup into the food processor. Process until the mixture is a pale yellow and thickened.
5. Turn off the food processor to add the raspberries, salt, and lemon juice, and then process until the raspberries are pureed and the mixture is smooth.
6. (Optional) If you wish to remove the seeds, pour the mixture through a strainer. I prefer to keep the seeds.
7. Stir in the half-and-half.
8. Cover tightly and refrigerate until cold or overnight.
9. Stir the chilled mixture. Next, either run it through your ice cream machine according to its instructions, possibly in two batches, or explore one of the alternative four methods above.
10. Enjoy! Your final ice cream will be soft even after freezing overnight.

DATE COMPLETED:

_____

FLAVOR(S)/METHOD:

_____

NOTES:

_____

_____

_____

_____

_____

_____

_____

_____

_____

_____

_____

4. PREPARE BROWNIES FROM SCRATCH

Grab the family homemade brownie recipe, solicit one from a friend, search for "easy brownie recipes" online, or try my favorite recipe below. The challenge today is to make brownies from scratch.

No cheating with a boxed brownie mix from the store! A friend's "recipe" that involves a store mix does not count. Brownies made from scratch are surprisingly simple and will reward you with a sense of pride for having crafted them.

HERE IS HOW I TEND TO PREPARE BROWNIES:

- 2 cups white sugar
- 1 1/2 cups all-purpose flour
- 1 cup butter, melted
- 4 eggs
- 1/2 cup cocoa powder
- 1 teaspoon vanilla extract
- 1/2 teaspoon baking powder
- 1/2 teaspoon salt

Optional: ½ cup of peanut butter chips (or chopped wal-nuts, or craisins, or chocolate chips, or whatever fun ingredient you have on hand and you're willing to try as a toss-in. Think of these like pancakes where you get the base batter down and experiment with whatever might pair well).

1. Preheat the oven to 350 degrees F. Grease an 8 x 8-inch pan.
2. Combine sugar, flour, butter, eggs, cocoa powder, vanilla extract, baking powder, and salt in a large bowl.
3. Fold in whatever adventurous ingredient you're folding in, if any.
4. Spread the batter into the prepared pan.
5. Bake about 20 to 30 minutes in the preheated oven until top is dry and edges have started to pull away from the sides of the pan. Cool completely before slicing into squares.

DATE COMPLETED:

_____

RECIPE SOURCE (for when you want to make it again):

_____

NOTES:

_____

_____

_____

_____

_____

_____

_____

_____

_____

_____

5. BLEND A HOMEMADE SMOOTHIE

Any time of year, and especially in summer, a homemade smoothie feels like dessert masquerading as breakfast or a snack. It's a solid mood booster, can be nutritious, and is surprisingly easy to prepare.

Seek inspiration for recipes online or make use of the fresh or frozen produce you have on hand.

Pull out your blender and start with ice as a base. Layer on fresh or frozen fruit that appeals to you, perhaps add some spinach or kale for extra nutrients. Top it off with your preferred juice and blend. Enjoy as a breakfast to start your day or as a late morning or afternoon snack.

Savor the boost that comes along with this treat.

FOR ADDITIONAL INSPIRATION, HERE IS THE RECIPE FOR MY GO-TO SMOOTHIE:

- 1 cup of frozen strawberries
- 1 cup of frozen mixed berries (blackberries, blue-berries, raspberries)
- 1 fresh banana
- Handful (or two) of spinach

- 1-2 cups of orange juice (passionfruit juice also works well)
- Ice

1. Add ice to blender so it fills roughly 1/3 of the pitcher.
2. Add berries, banana, spinach.
3. Pour orange or passionfruit juice until you achieve a solid base of liquid for the mixture to blend.
4. Blend the mixture. Add more juice as needed to blend successfully and reach a drinkable consistency.

DATE COMPLETED:

_____

SMOOTHIE INGREDIENTS USED:

_____

NOTES:

_____

_____

_____

_____

_____

_____

_____

_____

_____

_____

6. PICK YOUR OWN PRODUCE

Identify what is in-season and growing locally, find a farm within driving distance, and make a day of it. Pick your own strawberries, peaches, apples, blueberries, raspberries, or anything else you have access to that sounds appealing. Dig peanuts or potatoes. Pick arugula or fresh spinach.

You will reap the benefits of physical movement, consuming fresh produce, and you will have the option of turning this into a bonding experience with family or friends.

DATE COMPLETED:

_____

VENUE:

_____

PRODUCE PICKED:

_____

NOTES:

_____

_____

_____

_____

_____

_____

_____

_____

7. ATTEND A FOOD OR BEVERAGE FESTIVAL

Is your town throwing a pretzel party? A chowder fest? Pierogies gathering? Gingerbread house competition? How about a county or state fair? Seek out the fun event and sample the fare.

To go the extra mile, sign up for a competition. Make your best pierogies, build a gingerbread architectural marvel, or enter those brownies you just made from scratch.

If you consume alcohol, get tickets for a beer or wine festival. In winter, look for an eggnog crawl. Make a toast to you and your abundance of free time. Just remember to drink responsibly and plan ahead for transportation.

NOTE: Those in unemployment may be more likely than their employed-selves to experience depression, which may lead to easier overindulge in alcohol or other substance abuse. Today's mission is *not* about getting hammered (in fact, none of these missions are); it is about raising a glass in the name of fun and relaxation. Unwind and be present as you enjoy yourself responsibly.

DATE COMPLETED:

_____

FESTIVAL DETAILS AND IMPRESSIONS:

_____

_____

_____

_____

_____

_____

_____

_____

_____

_____

_____

8.   ORDER A FLIGHT

Today's mission creates space for you to discover new flavors. If you consume alcohol, try a new vineyard or restaurant offering a wine flight. If you normally gravitate toward only a chardonnay, sample the sauvignon blanc, pinot grigio, or viognier. If you are firmly a cabernet sauvignon lover, try the shiraz, pinot noir, or zinfandel instead.

Prefer beer? Same idea, but head to a local brewery. Push yourself outside of your normal lager, porter, or IPA mold. Aim for the lemon blueberry sour or the mango Kolsch. Try the chocolate stout or the peanut butter porter.

It's okay if you hate the new beverages you try. The magic from this comes from expanding your mind, palate, and experience. Besides, once you have tried the new flavors, you can always treat yourself to your normal merlot or IPA and all will be right with the world again.

Taking kids with you? Some vineyards offer juice flights with food pairings.

For teetotalers, consider trying a new mocktail at a restaurant. Or concoct your own new beverage at home.

Pair your drinks of choice with tasty snacks and enjoy!

Again, remember to drink responsibly and plan ahead for transportation.

DATE COMPLETED:

_____

VENUE:

_____

IMPRESSIONS OF EACH SAMPLE IN THE FLIGHT:

_____

_____

_____

_____

_____

_____

_____

_____

_____

_____

9. HAVE A PICNIC

Get outside for a meal. Today you have the option to be solitary or in the company of others. If you prefer going this solo, embrace the time to reflect in silence and meditate if that suits you. Alternatively, leverage the time to plan a connective lunch or dinner with your kids, friends, spouse or partner, siblings, or other family.

Prepare homemade deli sandwiches, pasta salad, iced tea, or whatever picnic food appeals to you.

Grab a blanket and your culinary delights. Consider all five of your senses as you notice what's happening around you. Savor the tastes and aromas of the foods you have prepared. Take in the views and sounds of nature. Mindfully observe the feel of the blanket, the wind against your skin, or the grass under your bare toes. Be fully present.

DATE COMPLETED:

_____

NOTES ABOUT THE PICNIC:

_____

_____

_____

_____

_____

_____

_____

_____

_____

_____

_____

_____

10. MASTER THE INSTANT POT

Or air fryer or slow cooker or any other cooking gadget you bought during the pandemic and intended to use regularly, but instead sits neglected on your bottom cabinet shelf.

Pick a new recipe intended for preparation in your kitchen equipment of choice. Be bold and daring—endeavor to make a chickpea biryani instead of a vegetable soup. If it works, you have added to your repertoire; if it doesn't, you have a good story to tell along with a good laugh.

DATE COMPLETED:

_____

EQUIPMENT:

_____

RECIPE SELECTED:

_____

NOTES:

_____

_____

_____

_____

_____

_____

_____

_____

11. MAKE YOUR OWN VANILLA EXTRACT

For this mission, you'll need 4 oz or 8 oz glass bottles, vanilla bean sticks, and vodka. Sterilize the bottles and caps, carefully slice each vanilla bean stick open length-wise with a sharp knife and drop one or two into each sterilized bottle. Use a funnel to add vodka filling to the top. Cap and label the bottles. Store in a cool, dark place; shake bottles once or twice a week. Let the vanilla and vodka combo infuse for a minimum of three months before using. Six to 12 months is often optimal.

Plan now and this can serve as holiday gifts or party favors at a future event. Design a fun label to showcase the mag-nificence of your creation (see #95, Digital Creation).

Experiment with several types of vanilla beans — Mada-gascar and Tahitian, for example. Be sure to label every-thing clearly so you can identify and remember which you like best.

DATE COMPLETED:

_____

TYPE(S) OF BEANS:

_____

BRAND OF VODKA:

_____

BOTTLING DATE AND NOTES:

_____

_____

_____

_____

_____

_____

_____

_____

_____

12. CREATE YOUR OWN HOT SAUCE

Whether or not you intend to consume the end product, try your hand at a homemade hot sauce recipe. The process is far simpler than you might expect and the end result is generally better than what you can purchase at the grocery store. High level, this involves fermenting peppers, then blending them with a few other tasty ingredients like garlic and salt.

If hot sauce is not your thing, give your prized accomplishment to friends or family members. But keep an open mind, maybe this will open your palate to it. And remember, hot sauce does not have to sear your tongue—aim to develop a mild recipe if that suits you.

Here's an exciting twist for this chapter. While developing this chapter, I was on a road trip in North Carolina, where I connected with an owner of Three Sisters Farm from Needville, Texas. These sisters not only make their own hot sauce, they grow their own peppers and sell the finished product at local markets and their roadside stand.

Hearing about this book, they enthusiastically agreed to share their recipe here for you to try. I have since tried my hand at their recipe using Poblano, Fresno, and Serrano peppers (three separate batches). Consider combining this with the Farmers' Market mission to purchase your fresh peppers.

THREE SISTERS FARM HOT SAUCE RECIPE

- 1 pound fresh peppers of your choice
- 2 Tbsps. canning salt (Kosher salt may be substituted)
- White or apple cider vinegar (5% acidity) (about 2 cups)

Yield: Appx. 24 fl. oz.

PART 1:

1. Wash and remove the cap and stem of peppers.
2. Add to blender (Three Sisters Farm uses a Vitamix) in stages and blend to a coarse purée.
3. Add salt and blend to a smoother purée.
4. Empty contents into a quart jar and fill with the vinegar of your choice. The jar must be full.
5. Seal with a nonreactive lid. Add label with date and ingredient list.
6. Shake or stir daily for at least 2 weeks, longer is okay. The vinegar will absorb the flavor of the other ingredients.

PART 2:

7. After two weeks or so, return contents to the blender and run on high for 2 minutes.

8. Pour through a stainless-steel strainer to remove some of the solids. This will include the ground-up seed casings, which could give a bitter flavor if not strained. Some pepper solids will remain in the remaining sauce. The amount will vary by pepper variety.

9. Heat to boiling in a stainless steel pot and boil (high simmer) uncovered, stirring regularly, for 2 minutes, or until foam subsides. Serranos are particularly foamy.

10. Pour into glass bottles or jars using a stainless steel or plastic funnel.

IMPORTANT NOTES:

1. Feel free to adjust the flavor in Part 1 of the recipe with sugar, balsamic vinegar, mixed peppers, herbs, and other spices.

2. Since you are essentially working with a flavored vinegar, do *not* use aluminum pots or utensils! Chemical reactions will ultimately lead to dissolved aluminum, which is not safe to consume.

3. While hot sauce is reasonably shelf stable, it will last longer and keep its original color if refrigerated after opening. Shake before using.

4. Prepare each batch in its own jar, even if processing multiple pounds. Doing the second blend on high speed requires plenty of room in the blender. All batches can be strained into the same pot for cooking off.

DATE COMPLETED:

_____

YOUR NOTES ABOUT THE RECIPE:

_____

_____

_____

_____

_____

_____

_____

_____

_____

_____

_____

13. VISIT A FARMERS' MARKET

Seek out a local farmers' market. Explore the fresh produce, newly baked bread, and locally sourced honey. Purchase at least one vegetable or fruit for consumption that day. Or, gather your fresh peppers for homemade hot sauce.

The important objective today is to slow down and notice the vibrant colors and pronounced aromas surrounding you. You may also want to embrace this as an opportunity to interact with new people.

DATE COMPLETED:

_____

PURCHASE(S):

_____

_____

REFLECTIONS:

_____

_____

_____

_____

_____

_____

_____

_____

_____

_____

_____

14. SAMPLE OLIVE OIL / VINEGAR

If you have specialty shops nearby that offer olive oil or balsamic vinegar tastings, make an intentional event of it. Arrive with an open mind to sample oils and vinegars that might sound outright unappealing to you. Lavender vinegar or blood orange olive oil? Trust me, they are worth a try.

To start inspiring this adventure, explore fruity flavors of blueberry, cranberry, strawberry, pomegranate, black cherry, or blackberry ginger vinegars. Perhaps a richer sweet is more your style—consider coconut, chocolate, or espresso. Leaning more earthy or umami? Try mushroom, hickory smoke, or teriyaki. Heat enthusiasts: the green chili, chipotle, cayenne, and habanero honey have your name on them. Other adventurers consider cinnamon pear, watermelon, Persian lime, or dill.

After all your adventurous sampling, be sure to patronize the shop with at least one interesting new bottle that catches your fancy. Take home several if your wallet can handle it.

ALTERNATIVE: INFUSE YOUR OWN

If you do not have access to specialty olive oil shops, consider infusing your own herb vinegar. Your base vinegar can pretty much be whatever you have on hand—apple cider vinegar, red wine vinegar, rice vinegar, balsamic, or white to name a few.

Herb possibilities run the gamut as well—think basil, chives, lavender, sage, rosemary, fennel as starting examples.

- 2 cups of fresh herbs
- 4 cloves of garlic (peeled, whole)
- 4 cups of vinegar

1. Rinse your herbs of choice and dry gently between two paper towels.
2. Crush the herbs lightly to release their flavor. Place into a glass jar with garlic cloves.
3. Pour vinegar over the herbs and garlic, place a piece of plastic wrap covering the opening of the jar before affixing the jar's lid.
4. Store for two weeks at room temperature out of the sun's reach—a dark cabinet is great.
5. Once you have reached the desired taste, strain vinegar into a bottle and discard the spent herbs and garlic. Store tightly covered.
6. Enjoy!

DATE COMPLETED:

_____

PURCHASE(S) / CREATION(S):

_____

_____

REFLECTIONS:

_____

_____

_____

_____

_____

_____

_____

_____

_____

15. LEARN TO MAKE COFFEE A NEW WAY

I get that not everyone drinks coffee. I am not one of those people. For those of us who regularly consume coffee or a hot beverage in the morning, it's part of a ritual. Holding the mug, taking a sip of divine hot liquid, inhaling the aroma. Removing that from our morning is inconceivable. Let's embrace the daily ritual but expand our exploration with a twist just for today.

If you usually purchase your coffee out of the house, pivot that routine immediately. The amount of money you will save in the long run by preparing your own coffee will be worth any initial investment in supplies. Hemorrhaging cash when you are employed is a luxurious option. Now, if something needs to give in your budget, this is a great place to start. Determine if you would like a drip-style coffee pot or something fancier. Make the purchase and learn the new equipment.

For those already making your own coffee, if you always head immediately to the one-cup coffee maker, instead endeavor to prepare for yourself coffee via a French press or pour over. Alternatively, whip up a homemade latte or cappuccino if you have the equipment.

Take some time to explore beans from different regions of the world.

If your newly tried method appeals, keep at it. If you prefer the normal, return to that tomorrow. For today, savor your coffee made differently from the norm.

NOTES ON BEANS:

_____

_____

_____

_____

DATE COMPLETED:

_____

NOTES ON COFFEE METHOD:

_____

_____

_____

_____

OTHER REFLECTIONS:

_____

_____

_____

_____

CONNECT

Extroverts and introverts unite! Irrespective of where you draw your energy, we all have the need for connection. Now, with the gift of time, you can tend to relationships that may have fallen by the wayside when you were eyeball deep in PowerPoint decks and spreadsheets. While our inclination may be to curl up into a ball and hide under the covers, I urge you to reconsider that tendency. Connections are arguably more important at this time.

Here, prepare to cultivate new relationships. Who knows? One of these missions may even lead to a contact at your dream company. Not the very first mission, but others deeper in this section may be the key.

16. SPEND MORE TIME WITH YOUR KIDS

For those with children, this is, hands down, the most important suggestion in the entire book. Consistently, people I interviewed emphasized how grateful they are in this time of unemployment to have more focused and quality time with their kids. I fully agree.

For those with kids living at home, say yes to their requests for shared activities. If they ask you to chaperone a school trip, draw together with sidewalk chalk, or play mini golf — say yes to all the things you have the ability to do.

If your kids do not approach you with ideas, offer your own suggestions for age-appropriate ways to connect with them. For younger kids, read to them, play together with their toys, or just cuddle.

For older kids, pull out a board game, take a family walk, make homemade ice cream together, or kick around a soccer ball. Make a conscious effort to get away from screens. Ask them to teach you something, invent a new game together, or tell a story in the round. Whatever your child or children's activities are, do that with them. See them and meet them where they are. Be sure to devote energy into your relationship with each of your children individually.

Grown kids? Plan an open-ended FaceTime, rather than just an allotted 30 minutes. Or, suggest binge watching a show with them — either remotely or in-person — that you haven't had time for until now.

If you don't have children, reach out to a niece or nephew you would like to get to know better.

Mindfully pause and be sure you are fully present. This is critical. Time passes quickly; make the most of it.

Fill this entire page. Relish the time.

DATE COMPLETED:

_____

ACTIVITIES ENJOYED:

_____

_____

_____

_____

REFLECTIONS:

_____

_____

_____

_____

_____

_____

_____

_____

17. CONNECT MORE DEEPLY WITH YOUR SPOUSE OR PARTNER

If you're in a committed relationship, now is a perfect time to be present. See your person where they are. Assuming you like your life partner and you are in a healthy relationship, spend more time with them. Support them and also lean on them as much as you need right now. Enjoy a date night as often as schedules and budget allows.

Perhaps now you can also do things for them that you normally would not have had the time to do. For example, prepare their favorite lemon bars as a surprise treat, actively listen to them, and curiously ask questions to understand what's processing through their mind. Consider taking on one of their household chores (throw standard gender roles out the window).

Chores and household maintenance aside, pick an activity or adventure you both enjoy. Or, stretch to meet them in their world. If they're a rock climber and you normally prefer to keep your feet firmly on the ground, earn bonus points for joining them on and actively participating in a climbing trip outdoors.

The important objective is to be present and connect meaningfully, irrespective of how you choose to accomplish that.

DATE COMPLETED:

_____

ACTIVITIES EXPLORED:

_____

_____

_____

_____

REFLECTIONS:

_____

_____

_____

_____

_____

_____

_____

_____

18. MAKE TIME FOR EXTENDED FAMILY

Remember that family member you were close with once upon a time? Maybe time with a sibling or perhaps with a favorite aunt or uncle would recharge you. A busy work schedule may have contributed to your drifting apart. Let's change that.

Initiate a renewed connection through a call, text, or email. Set a date and place to get together and stick to the plan.

My personal journey included multiple days with two cousins on separate weekends. Additionally, my brother stayed with me for several weeks of playing board games, sightseeing, cooking, and helping with projects around the house.

You don't need to invite family to move in. But do make plans to see that individual in-person. This get-together can include additional people, but try to keep the gathering small enough that you can meaningfully connect with your key person.

DATE COMPLETED:

_____

WHO:

_____

WHEN:

_____

WHERE:

_____

REFLECTIONS:

_____

_____

_____

_____

_____

_____

19. REACH OUT TO A FRIEND

When you were head-down in your job, you may have had just enough energy to stay connected with your immediate household, while activities with friends surfaced as a rare treat.

Who do you miss? Whose company would you enjoy over a walk, a cup of coffee, or a lunch? Who haven't you seen in over a year? Reach out even if it's for a video chat.

For the overachievers out there, write down three people and schedule get-togethers with each one to take place over the course of the next month. Too much of a stretch? Just make one connection.

DATE COMPLETED:

_____

PERSON 1:

_____

PERSON 1 DATE:

_____

PERSON 1 ACTIVITY:

_____

_____

_____

_____

_____

PERSON 2:

_____

PERSON 2 DATE:

_____

PERSON 2 ACTIVITY:

_____

_____

_____

_____

_____

PERSON 3:

_____

PERSON 3 DATE:

_____

PERSON 3 ACTIVITY:

_____

_____

_____

_____

20. GET TO KNOW A NEIGHBOR

It's easy to wave at people in your neighborhood and say hello as you hurriedly continue on your way. Today, pause and initiate a conversation with one of your neighbors. Meaningfully connect. Look them in the eye. Notice— what color are their eyes?

Avoid commenting on the weather. Focus instead on inquiring about their family, pets, property updates, hobbies, or community happenings. Keep the discussion positive, focused on them. As per normal conversation etiquette, it's good balance to include personal commentary and stories, but start with focus on your neighbor. Follow up with them later for updates on anything that you learned about them.

DATE COMPLETED:

_____

NEIGHBOR:

_____

_____

FOLLOW-UP(S):

_____

_____

REFLECTIONS:

_____

_____

_____

_____

_____

_____

_____

21. WRITE A LETTER

Today's mission returns us to the pre-digital age. Grab a piece of actual stationary if you have it, lined or computer paper if you don't, and a pen. Identify someone who has made a positive impact on you whom you would like to thank. Before putting pen to paper, formulate your thoughts. What do you admire about the person? What are positive memories you shared together? How did they affect your trajectory?

Be creative. Perhaps it's a former teacher or professor who inspired the skills for your career path. Or, maybe a former boss who guided and developed you over the years. Consider thanking your grocery cashier who consistently ensures solid care of your purchases through the checkout process. Or write to an elderly relative who helped shape you in your formative years.

Maybe you have never met your recipient; leverage the art of the letter to introduce yourself and establish contact.

I directed my first letter to the current owners of my childhood home. I applauded several improvements they made to the exterior, reflected on how the house looked inside at the time of my occupancy, and offered contact information should they be curious to see decades-old pictures of their property. To my delight, the owners, who have lived at the house for over thirty years, sent me a lovely hand-written letter back. What a lift to my day to read about interior updates and to hear about how my former neighbors, still there, are doing.

I offer this anecdote as a way to stretch your thinking beyond a letter to the usual suspects. I'm sure those individuals (parents, partner, best friend) will enjoy one as well. Write several in accordance with your level of genuine enthusiasm.

Craft your letter(s), locate address(es), and drop your heartfelt creation in the mail for tomorrow's pickup. If you're opting for the grocery cashier or other service industry support, don't be creepy with locating their address—hand deliver it with your next checkout.

DATE COMPLETED:

_____

LETTER RECIPIENT(S):

_____

_____

_____

_____

_____

_____

_____

_____

_____

_____

_____

_____

22. VOLUNTEER

Volunteering offers an opportunity to connect with other people, give back to your community, and seek relief from your own worries.

Begin by identifying which causes are most important to you. If you love dogs, reach out to your community animal shelter to see if you can help walk dogs or simply offer affection or other care to the animals. If food insecurity is high on your list, check out local food pantries or homeless shelters and serve a meal or two. Many nonprofits will accept as many or as few hours as you wish to devote.

If you have kids still in school, see if their teachers need any support. Perhaps you can assist with an extracurricular activity such as sports, robotics, or knitting club. Volunteer in the school library, lead a classroom party, or help facilitate lunch.

Middle schools and high schools often seek tutors, and they may even pay you a few dollars for your efforts. While not strictly volunteering, it is an exercise in raising your hand to be involved in the community.

Another possibility is to join a committee. Spearhead a community event or offer an extra set of hands at an event in motion. Local businesses may seek volunteers to help with a one-time or seasonal event such as a fair, craft show, or race.

If your journey coincides with an election cycle, work the polls or participate in a get-out-the-vote campaign.

If you receive great intrinsic value from volunteering, by all means, continue. But if this offers only a temporary reward, set a limit on how many hours you are willing to devote, and stick to it. Be careful not to let this turn into a huge commitment that distracts from critical job searching time. Remember this is all a balance.

DATE COMPLETED:

_____

ORGANIZATION(S) SUPPORTED:

_____

_____

REFLECTIONS:

_____

_____

_____

_____

_____

_____

_____

_____

_____

_____

23. DONATE BLOOD / PLATELETS

Perhaps you weren't expecting to see donating blood in the connection chapter. Community support, interactions inherent in the experience, and the potential to save a life all sweep together into what I consider to be a connective, supportive experience.

This suggestion emerged from one of my peers in the insights industry who shared that donating platelets as often as guidelines permit enables her to stay grounded. She reflects, "This 'gift' of time was not by my choice, but if others can benefit, then there is something good to be taken from the whole experience."

Her new habit is altruistic toward her community in a way that might be overlooked.

According to the American Red Cross, platelet donations benefit "Cancer patients, those receiving organ or bone marrow transplants, victims of traumatic injuries, and patients undergoing open heart surgery." Expect to carve out approximately one hour for whole blood and three hours for platelet donations.

If you are able, search for blood drives in your neighborhood or an American Red Cross donation center.

If you're unable to donate blood, consider ways to support a similar effort in your community. For instance, leverage social media to spread the word about local blood drives or consider volunteering to assist with event coordination, checking donors in, or shuttling post-donation snacks.

DATE COMPLETED:

_____

REFLECTIONS:

_____

_____

_____

_____

_____

_____

_____

_____

_____

_____

_____

_____

24. PERFORM A RANDOM ACT OF KINDNESS

Help carry someone's groceries, take in mail and packages for a traveling neighbor, hold the door, offer to babysit, pick up litter, or pay a compliment.

If the opportunity arises and you have the physical ability, shovel the walkway of the property next to you or mow the lawn of a neighbor who you know needs the help. If you know a colleague or friend who is struggling or could use support, prepare a meal for their family.

Whatever you choose to do, smile and feel the benefits of lending a hand.

DATE COMPLETED:

_____

ACTS OF KINDNESS REFLECTIONS:

_____

_____

_____

_____

_____

_____

_____

_____

_____

_____

_____

_____

25. EXPAND YOUR PROFESSIONAL NETWORK

Today's mission encourages you to make meaningful professional connections.

If your LinkedIn network is anything like mine, you have throngs of first connections you have no recollection of meeting. Scroll through them and pick a contact with something interesting in their background. Perhaps you enjoy a similar hobby or maybe their banner photo includes an image that raises a question about what inspired the selection. Send them a message noting what piqued your interest and suggest grabbing 30 minutes in the next week to connect by video. If the person lives nearby, offer to meet in-person for coffee or lunch.

Next, choose a second person, one with whom you have an academic connection. When you initiate contact, assuming you know them, open by recounting a positive anecdote from your school days. Invite them to join you in a video catch-up.

Finally, choose a third person, and this time, aim for someone with a high-level position at your dream company. Check out their recent posts, published articles, and video interviews. As you initiate contact, consider commenting on their published content that you found most meaning-ful. Propose grabbing a moment at their convenience for an informational interview.

You can, of course, select any three people from your net-work and send a custom message, but gamifying the rules will make it more interesting.

DATE COMPLETED:

_____

PERSON 1:

_____

PERSON 1 NOTES:

_____

_____

_____

_____

_____

PERSON 2:

_____

PERSON 2 NOTES:

_____

_____

_____

_____

_____

_____

_____

PERSON 3:

_____

PERSON 3 NOTES:

_____

_____

_____

_____

_____

26. SET OTHER LINKEDIN GOALS

Set a specific goal on LinkedIn and a reasonable timeline to achieve it then get to work.

Perhaps you would like to earn a Voice badge. This is a virtual endorsement from LinkedIn that puts a spotlight on your skills and knowledge, perhaps enhancing credibility. Devote an afternoon to commenting on the necessary posts then celebrate in a few days when your reward comes through.

Maybe you desire to reach a certain number of connections. Set a timeline including a goal of connecting with x number of people per week. But be sure to achieve it with meaningful connections from your industry, educational institutions, or target companies, rather than chasing empty numbers fueled solely by LinkedIn's algorithms.

Another potential goal is to take the stage in a LinkedIn Live event. Similar to speaking in-person at a conference, this is a virtual opportunity to provide content to your industry through a presentation or live conversation. Design your topic, create the event, invite your newly expanded network, and have fun with it.

You are not limited to these specific ideas. Set any positive LinkedIn goal and go after it.

DATE COMPLETED:

_____

GOAL SELECTED:

_____

_____

STRATEGY TO ACHIEVE IT:

_____

_____

_____

_____

_____

_____

_____

_____

_____

27. JOIN A NETWORKING GROUP

Isolation in unemployment is real. Post-pandemic, virtual connections make it easier to avoid isolation. Take advantage of this paradigm shift by staying connected with other adults and finding fun ways to stay sharp and in the game.

If possible, join a local group that meets in-person. Attend at least one event. If in-person groups are sparse, seek professional groups that meet virtually.

Join several groups if you have the energy and enthusiasm for nurturing all the new relationships. You are not required to attend every single meeting. Rather, joining affords you the option to participate as often or as little as you like. Commit to a minimum of one meeting per month and if you are inspired to attend more often, go for it.

Following each of your networking meetings, send a customized outreach connecting with new contacts on LinkedIn. Remind them of where you met and suggest a one-on-one meeting virtually to continue the relationship. Approach at least one, but aim for three new contacts from each group meeting.

DATE COMPLETED:

_____

GROUP(S) JOINED:

_____

_____

_____

OTHER GROUP POSSIBILITIES:

_____

_____

_____

_____

_____

_____

_____

28. ATTEND A FREE OR LOW-COST CONFERENCE

Stay vigilant to free or very low-cost events that put you in the same room as potential future employers. Content covered at the event can help keep you sharp with the latest happenings in your industry. And potential contacts could connect you with your next role. Plus, the change of venue, the act of dressing up, and the variety of food (even if unappetizing) can all serve to boost your mood and perspective.

Search for conferences in your city or an easy trip from your home. Ask friends and former colleagues for recommendations. Seek discounts when possible. One of the networking groups you joined from the last mission may even raffle off free passes to industry conferences.

Perhaps you can raise your hand to present at a conference, which usually lands you free entry into the event. A speaking engagement offers the added benefit of yielding even more eyeballs on you. This, in turn, makes you more approachable in the cocktail networking sessions and gives you another positive use of time as you prepare for the event.

Aim for a minimum of three new contacts to follow up with individually outside of the event.

DATE COMPLETED:

CONFERENCE(S):

---

29. ESTABLISH AN ACCOUNTABILITY PARTNER

Somewhere in the sea of endless networking calls, you will find someone who inspires you. When you discover that you inspire them as well, you have found your account-ability partner.

For greatest impact, meet regularly — weekly or every other week tend to function best. You and your partner can use the time however you would like, but the idea is to share goals you each intend to achieve between that call and the next meeting.

At the subsequent meeting, you each reflect upon how much you have accomplished toward your original goals and set new goals for the next time period. The mere act of having to answer to another person can increase your likelihood of staying driven and continuing to accomplish them.

Be each other's cheerleaders and champions. Commit to a minimum of four sessions together and evaluate whether this feels like a good use of time, whether the spirit of it is good but you need a new partner, or whether this strategy isn't a fit for you.

DATE COMPLETED:

_____

ACCOUNTABILITY PARTNER:

_____

_____

THOUGHTS:

_____

_____

_____

_____

_____

_____

_____

_____

_____

_____

30. BINGE A SHOW

Yes. You read that correctly. Give yourself permission to binge one season of one show. Try to limit your TV time so you're not on the sofa for a solid 24 hours. But, if you need a day where you want to lay there for a few hours and eat chocolate chip cookie dough, take it.

Only do this once if possible. Or impose another limit like once per quarter. But, be easy on yourself when you embrace this mission.

Binging may feel better as a connective experience rather than a solitary one. If it feels good, include family in your binge so you can process through the content together.

DATE COMPLETED:

_____

SHOW:

_____

_____

REFLECTIONS:

_____

_____

_____

_____

_____

_____

_____

ORGANIZE

Organizing offers numerous positive benefits. It inspires creativity, boosts productivity, and can improve your mental health. While certain things are outside of your control during this turbulent time, organizing is certainly within your control. So, let's get down to it!

31. ORGANIZE THE CLUTTER

Start with the biggest pain point. If you struggle with a junk drawer that you consistently add to but can never retrieve from it what you seek, that is your point of focus. If you have a bookcase that has been begging for reordering by category or author or function, go there.

Maybe your main living space overflows with knick-knacks and would benefit from boxing some up for storage or donation. Or consider whether a dresser needs some thinning out.

Once you have addressed the biggest issue, keep the momentum going and identify two more overflowing challenges, then go after them.

DATE COMPLETED:

_____

PAIN POINT 1 ADDRESSED:

_____

_____

_____

_____

PAIN POINT 2 ADDRESSED:

_____

_____

_____

_____

PAIN POINT 3 ADDRESSED:

_____

_____

_____

_____

32. CLEAN OUT A CLOSET

Identify the closet that has accumulated so many articles it no longer serves as functional. This could be the one in your bedroom housing your clothes. It could be your hallway closet where you have taken to storing sports equipment that you don't touch on a regular basis, shoes that have holes in them, and a collection of hats large enough to shield the sun from an entire village.

Pick the closet most in need of attention. Next, sort through piles for donation, trash, and other storage areas. Organize the remaining items and relish your newly usable space.

Remember to take note of all donations and claim the benefit at tax time. Intrinsic and financial benefits abound on this.

DATE COMPLETED:

_____

CLOSET TACKLED:

_____

NOTES:

_____

_____

_____

_____

_____

_____

_____

_____

_____

_____

33. SELL UNWANTED ITEMS

Have a treadmill that you never use taking up space? What about a piece of furniture you acquired along life's journey that no longer aligns with Current You?

Take a hard look at those collector's items laying around your house: baseball cards, vintage LEGO sets, porcelain dolls, stamps, or whatever you have collected and are comfortable parting with emotionally. List them online for extra cash.

For everyday noncollector's items, either sell online or hold a yard sale. If the effort of listing the items isn't worth the cash, lean into decluttering and simply give them away.

DATE COMPLETED:

_____

NOTES:

_____

_____

_____

_____

_____

_____

_____

_____

_____

_____

_____

_____

34. TAKE UP A HOME IMPROVEMENT PROJECT

Today's mission could be something extremely minor or a larger project. Maybe you wish to upgrade cabinet knobs in the kitchen, restain a table, change a light fixture, or swap out a toilet flapper.

Larger projects might include repairing drywall or repainting a room. Maybe the fuchsia-colored guest room was not exactly your thing when you bought the place, but you never had time to change it out. Go pick an amazing color that suits you and spend a day or two prepping and painting.

If you decide to take on an even bigger project, go for it! Pick something within your abilities and budget that will improve your feelings about your home.

If you can do the work yourself, you will keep costs to a minimum, so that's our target during this period. If the project is beyond your abilities or current budget, today's mission is only to plan. Research contractors, materials, colors, and other logistics. Sketch out a full scheme. You'll be ready to go once your financial situation changes.

Whatever the project, this is your opportunity to eliminate any historical unrest and feel properly content in your own space.

DATE COMPLETED:

_____

HOME IMPROVEMENT PROJECTS COMPLETED OR PLANNED:

_____

_____

_____

NOTES:

_____

_____

_____

_____

_____

_____

_____

_____

35. SPIFF UP YOUR OUTSIDE

Sprucing up the outside of your home helps bring order to your house overall. Depending on the season, set out to mow the lawn, rake the leaves, mulch or weed the garden, power wash the sidewalk or house, touch up paint on the railing, or clean the mailbox. Pick the one area that demands the most attention and harness the momentum for the second most dire area.

If you don't have a yard or other exterior space, maybe your front door needs a new peephole, the windows need washing, or the lighting cleaned.

DATE COMPLETED:

_____

ACCOMPLISHMENT 1:

_____

ACCOMPLISHMENT 2:

_____

NOTES:

_____

_____

_____

_____

_____

_____

_____

36. MAKE A DIY CLEANER

Make yourself a cleaning solution using ingredients you may have around the house. With vinegar, baking soda, and an essential oil or two, you can produce an effective and nice-smelling cleaner.

Search online for "homemade cleaners using simple ingre-dients" and pick what inspires you—a cleaning scrub, a counter spray, a glass and window cleaner, or an air fresh-ener spray.

For an easy DIY freshener spray, combine ½ cup of vodka, 1.5 cups of water, and 10 to 12 drops of your favorite essential oil to a spray bottle; dispense as needed.

DATE COMPLETED:

_____

NOTES:

_____

_____

_____

_____

_____

_____

_____

_____

_____

_____

_____

37. GET YOUR PHYSICAL HEALTH ON

Once you have sorted out the particulars of where your health coverage will be coming from (COBRA, partner's plan, personal coverage), schedule all of those well checks you have been putting off. Start with a physical and dentist, then move on to specialist screenings. You have the time. Make use of it so your schedule is tidy when you resume working again.

DATE COMPLETED:

_____

APPOINTMENT TYPES AND DATES:

_____

_____

_____

_____

_____

_____

_____

_____

_____

_____

_____

_____

38. REEVALUATE SUBSCRIPTIONS

We have all signed up for things that make sense for us at the time or that we intended to use often. This is a perfect opportunity to examine all those prior choices and make strategic decisions about what you wish to continue.

Examples include:

☐ Streaming music (Spotify, Pandora, Amazon Music, Sirius XM, Apple Music)

☐ Audiobooks (Audible, Kobo)

☐ All streaming TV (Netflix, Hulu, etc.)

☐ Magazines (digital or paper)

☐ Newspapers (digital or paper)

☐ Meal kit boxes (Hello Fresh, Blue Apron, Dinnerly)

☐ Subscription boxes (pet, beauty, clothing)

☐ Cybersecurity upgrades

☐ Software subscriptions

☐ Blogs and podcasts (Patreon, Substack)

SAMPLING LIFE

☐ Online gaming services (Xbox Live, Playstation Plus)

☐ App upgrades (meditation, organizing, financial)

☐ Credit monitoring

☐ Delivery (DoorDash, GrubHub, Shipt, Instacart)

☐ Cloud storage

☐ Warehouse memberships (Costco, BJs)

☐ Gym memberships

☐ Other

DATE COMPLETED:

_____

NOTES FOR OTHER SUBSCRIPTIONS TO EVALU-ATE/ELIMINATE:

_____

_____

_____

_____

_____

_____

_____

_____

_____

_____

_____

39. EVALUATE SERVICE CONTRACTS

Take a look at all of the ongoing services you have established to maintain your home and life in general. Research alternatives that may provide the same or better quality for a lower price.

Examples include:

- ☐ Cell carrier
- ☐ Internet
- ☐ Home or renter's insurance
- ☐ Auto insurance
- ☐ Home alarm
- ☐ Trash collection
- ☐ Lawn contract
- ☐ HVAC contract
- ☐ Home repairs contracts (e.g., plumbing or electrician)
- ☐ Other

DATE COMPLETED:

_____

NOTES FOR OTHER SERVICES CHANGED:

_____

_____

_____

_____

_____

_____

_____

_____

_____

_____

_____

_____

40. REMOVE JUNK EMAIL

Look at the last 100 emails you haven't opened that origi-
nated from a store or service provider. Do you need them?
Do you want them? Keep what suits you, delete and
unsubscribe from the rest.

DATE COMPLETED:

_____

NOTES:

_____

_____

_____

_____

_____

_____

_____

_____

_____

_____

_____

41. ORGANIZE PAPER FILES

Go through your paper records: financial statements, insurance documents, utility bills, receipts, tax files, and other documents you have accumulated.

Sort out the older papers you no longer need to keep. Shred the sensitive information, recycle the nonsensitive info, and relish the additional drawer space.

DATE COMPLETED:

_____

NOTES:

_____

_____

_____

_____

_____

_____

_____

_____

_____

_____

_____

_____

42. ORGANIZE DIGITAL FILES

Go through your digital files. Ensure that documents are all filed under proper headers. If you want to get really particular, employ a systematic naming or tagging convention to all files.

Delete all unnecessary files, duplicate drafts, and other digital artifacts that you no longer need. Move items you do not access regularly, but wish to preserve for long-term storage on an external hard drive or flash drive.

To go the extra mile, organize digital photos as well.

This task can potentially be a large undertaking. Give yourself permission to break this into chunks and return to it as needed.

DATE COMPLETED:

NOTES:

---

43. EVALUATE YOUR SLEEP ROUTINE

It's possible your working self prioritized the demands of earning a paycheck over quality sleep. You may have carried out a sleep routine on autopilot, without pausing to consider its merits or benefits. Now, you have time to focus on such an integral part of wellness.

Research shows that a consistent sleep routine increases the likelihood of higher quality sleep. Your pre-bed ritual primes the brain for winding down. The benefits include increased cognitive function, lower stress, boosted immune system, improved mood, and lower risk of injuries. If you have a sleep routine that works for you, keep at it. If you have room for adjustments, develop a measurable action plan.

Reflect on your pre-bed ritual. Do you wind down with a set routine in the same sequence every night? Are you heading to bed at a consistent time? What can set your body up for a more restful night? Would stacking a new habit to your current habits benefit you? Try things such as taking a warm bath, stretching, focusing on breathing, meditating, or reading just prior to bed.

Write down three specific actions you will take each night before bed in support of the new routine. Commit to doing these every night for two weeks as you try them on for size.

DATE COMPLETED:

_____

CURRENT ROUTINE:

_____

_____

CHANGES TO TRY:

_____

_____

REFLECTIONS:

_____

_____

_____

_____

_____

_____

BE ACTIVE

Research consistently shows that movement is a plus for our physical and mental well-being. Right now is the perfect time to take up a new sport or activity you have always wanted to try. If you are already engaged in an activity you love, use the time to elevate your skills to a new level.

Here are a few activities you may not have considered. Modify or skip if any or all are not for you.

44. THROW A LEFT HOOK

Enjoy a sanctioned and controlled way to punch things. My case for boxing could stop right there, but it won't. Boxing will spice up your normal workout routine, tone your muscles, and let out steam. Stress relief along with a high number of calories burned makes this workout an elixir of sorts.

Many boxing gyms will permit one free trial class. Take advantage of that offering. You can usually borrow gloves for your trial, but be aware that the gloves you borrow will smell far worse than ones you own. I'm noting this so you don't judge the activity based on smell alone. Also come equipped with a pair of wraps. You will likely get a better price buying these outside of the gym.

No need to worry about taking an uppercut to the chin. Instead, take your stress out on a heavy bag and sweat for an hour without the risk of getting punched. You will sleep amazingly well that night.

Disclaimer: This workout may be addictive. Be prepared to want to return.

DATE COMPLETED:

_____

REFLECTIONS:

_____

_____

_____

_____

_____

_____

_____

_____

_____

_____

_____

45. PLAY AT YOUR LOCAL PARK

Fling on the swings and glide down the slide like you did as a kid. Hang on the monkey bars, teeter on the see-saw, and take advantage of all the customized fun available to you at your local park. As adults, we sometimes forget how much of a release swinging on a swing can be.

You can bring kids with you, other adults, or you can do this one solo. The key is to let loose and play (safely) with abandon. Who cares who's watching? Just be mindful to share the space with any kids who are angling for the equipment.

DATE COMPLETED:

_____

REFLECTIONS:

_____

_____

_____

_____

_____

_____

_____

_____

_____

_____

_____

46. LEARN THE THRILLER DANCE

Okay, so maybe this comes uniquely from my personal list. And, maybe it only holds generational appeal. While my goal was to master the *Thriller* dance, you do not need to select the same one.

Pick some choreography that appeals to you. Find a YouTube video that walks you through step-by-step, and devote an afternoon to it. The movement will be more fun than you expect. Give yourself permission to be all in.

Bonus points if you recruit others to join you in this quest. If your dance of choice involves different people moving at different times—like the zombies that swing from side to side at opposing times—do it! More people will up the challenge and improve the end result, particularly if you capture the final product on video.

DATE COMPLETED:

_____

DANCE CHOSEN:

_____

_____

REFLECTIONS:

_____

_____

_____

_____

_____

_____

_____

_____

_____

47. THROW A ROUND OF DISC GOLF

The day I was notified of my layoff, I closed my laptop and went for a walk around a nearby lake where I redis-covered an adjacent disc golf course. I immediately texted a former colleague who had taken up disc golf during his time of unemployment two years prior and set a time he could acquaint me with the game. I have since explored multiple courses, appreciating the white space the sport offers my mind in addition to the physical movement. It's worth a try.

Search for a local park that offers disc golf and go play a round. If you can throw a Frisbee, you can play this sport. Play proceeds much the way regular golf does, with play-ers using a driver disc from the tee, moving on to fair-ways, and finally using a putter disc when near the "hole," which is a metal basket. Trees and other natural obstacles like hills and streams make the journey to the hole more interesting. If you see an arrow, you are required to clear that mandatory marker in the noted direction rather than moving straight to the hole. A one-throw penalty is added for not successfully maneuvering the mando.

Many parks allow free entry, and I have yet to see required reservations for a tee time. Show up and play solo or with friends or family. Though, like golf, you will be expected to keep pace of play, so generally no more than four people on a hole at one time. If you have a bigger family or you're just moving at a slug's pace that day, be courteous and allow faster players to play through. Keep score, play as a scramble, or just throw for fun.

Before you head out, search online for low-cost starter sets that include a bag, driver, fairway discs, and putter. Trying this addictive and therapeutic sport requires minimal investment.

Once you have officially caught the disc golf bug, stretch by trying other parks for varied terrain and obstacles.

One last tip: Label all of your discs with your phone number so that you can be reunited with any that are lost. And if you recover someone else's disc, put the good karma out there and notify them.

DATE COMPLETED:

_____

REFLECTIONS:

_____

_____

_____

_____

_____

_____

_____

_____

_____

_____

_____

48. RELAX IN DOWN DOG

You don't need to be a yogi to reap the benefits of a yoga session. The stretching, and other large and small movements, will increase muscle strength and clear your mind.

If paying a yoga studio is unappealing or not an option, seek yoga practices online. Some free or low-cost apps allow a customized practice. You can opt to work on twists or backbends or breathing, for instance, and set the length of time you wish to devote. Voilà, a custom practice in your own home with all the benefits.

Also consider hot yoga. Many studios will allow new students to try one class free. Use it for this.

Search for *Bikram* or *hot yoga* in your area. Prepare to sweat, and check modesty at the door. Plan on a performance sports bra and wicking short shorts for women. Men, dress in as little clothing as appropriate. Bring water, a mat, a towel, and possibly a change of clothes. Also, not a terrible idea to have something to sit on in your car on the way home if you do not wish to continue sweating onto the seat.

Hydrate before and after and replenish with electrolytes. Hot yoga is especially enjoyable in winter.

If yoga bores you, look to tai chi, Krav Maga (more physically aggressive than yoga or tai chi), or another martial art.

If you have joint issues or are recovering from an injury, consider chair yoga. I leaned into chair yoga as an option when I broke my wrist a few years ago and was able to reap many benefits of yoga without having to put stress on my healing bones.

Namaste.

DATE COMPLETED:

_____

REFLECTIONS:

_____

_____

_____

_____

_____

_____

_____

_____

_____

_____

_____

_____

49. PLANT FLOWERS OR VEGETABLE SEEDS/BULBS

Select a flower that makes you smile and plant it in your garden. If you don't have a garden, plant it in a pot that lives outside or inside with you.

Not a flower fan? Plant some veggies instead. Either stay tried and true to vegetables you know you like and will consume often or be adventurous with a new vegetable.

Alternatively, consider planting herbs. Fresh rosemary, basil, or mint can be nice enhancements to your prepared dishes.

No matter which option you choose, get your hands dirty. Let the soil be part of your journey that later gives you beauty or nourishment or both.

DATE COMPLETED:

_____

DETAILS ON PLANTING:

_____

_____

_____

_____

_____

_____

_____

_____

_____

_____

_____

_____

50. PLAY CATCH

Get outdoors and throw a frisbee or toss a ball with your kids, a friend, or a partner.

For a minimum of 10 minutes, run and throw like you did as a kid. Be 100% present.

DATE COMPLETED:

_____

REFLECTIONS:

_____

_____

_____

_____

_____

_____

_____

_____

_____

_____

_____

_____

51. SWING A RACKET

Do you have a tennis racket or badminton or racquetball set gathering dust in your closet? Take it out! Have you ever tried pickleball? A starter set is inexpensive.

Head to a public tennis or pickleball court. For racquetball, seek a venue that offers low-cost court fees.

Heck, turn this into four suggestions if you'd like and take these on over the course of four days.

☐ Badminton date:_____

☐ Pickleball date: _____

☐ Racquetball date: _____

☐ Tennis date:_____

You can, but do not need to keep score. Play for at least 30 minutes. If you don't have a companion top-of-mind to recruit as an opponent, seek a court with a solid wall on one end so you can practice your tennis or pickleball swing solo.

DATE COMPLETED:

_____

REFLECTIONS:

_____

_____

_____

_____

_____

_____

_____

_____

_____

_____

_____

_____

52. RALLY A VOLLEYBALL

This is a low-cost sport to take up. All you need is a ball and a net and some open space. If not your yard, head to a nearby park or beach.

Grab a ball and a few players and hit around. Play at least one full game.

DATE COMPLETED:

_____

REFLECTIONS:

_____

_____

_____

_____

_____

_____

_____

_____

_____

_____

_____

_____

53. TOSS CORNHOLE

If you don't own a set, look into borrowing one, buying secondhand, or building a set. Building counts as two activity completions.

If you have no desire to own a set, look to local restaurants that might offer free use of their sets for patrons. Grab a drink and some appetizers and enjoy the friendly competition.

DATE COMPLETED:

_____

REFLECTIONS:

_____

_____

_____

_____

_____

_____

_____

_____

_____

_____

_____

_____

54. PLAY CROQUET

Like cornhole, if you don't already own a croquet set, aim to find one secondhand or purchase one new if you think you might enjoy the investment.

For extra fun, play it up by donning "proper" croquet attire—perhaps a white sundress, fedora, plaid pants, or an argyle vest. Bring in some lemonade, an outdoor cocktail, or another festive beverage to complete the experience.

For my family croquet competitions, I enjoyed preparing pineapple margaritas. While this may have absolutely nothing to do with croquet, it offers a cocktail option outside of the usual suspects, is easy to make, and accompanies a floppy sunhat well as an outdoor accessory.

TO MAKE A PINEAPPLE MARGARITA:

- Lime zest
- Salt (optional)
- Pineapple chunks
- 1 oz. fresh lime juice
- 1 oz. pineapple juice

- 1 oz. tequila
- 1 oz. triple sec
- ¾ oz. simple syrup

1. Rub a lime wedge along the rim of an 8 oz. glass. Dip rim into salt and lime zest to coat. Set aside.
2. Muddle six small pineapple chunks, lime juice, and pineapple juice in a cocktail shaker.
3. Add ice cubes to the shaker, then add tequila, triple sec, and simple syrup. Cover and shake well.
4. Fill prepared glass with ice cubes; strain drink into glass.
5. Garnish with fresh pineapple chunk.

DATE COMPLETED:

_____

REFLECTIONS:

_____

_____

_____

_____

_____

_____

_____

_____

_____

_____

_____

_____

55. SHOOT POOL

Regular pool shark? Go play your game.

New to pool? Some establishments offer lessons or quick tutorials. YouTube can also be a good resource to get you started.

Somewhere in between? Just go have fun.

DATE COMPLETED:

_____

REFLECTIONS:

_____

_____

_____

_____

_____

_____

_____

_____

_____

_____

_____

56. SLIDE AIR HOCKEY OR TOSS SKEE-BALL

Head to an arcade and play like you did as a child. If you didn't play as a child, still put yourself in those shoes. If you need to, predetermine a budget for this activity and stick to it. Arcade play can be addictive.

DATE COMPLETED:

_____

REFLECTIONS:

_____

_____

_____

_____

_____

_____

_____

_____

_____

_____

_____

_____

57. THROW DARTS

Make use of a personal dart board or head to a local estab-lishment that offers darts. Play for fun or competitively.

Challenge yourself to at least two different types of games. Perhaps Around the World and Cricket to get you started.

DATE COMPLETED:

_____

REFLECTIONS:

_____

_____

_____

_____

_____

_____

_____

_____

_____

_____

_____

_____

58. ROLL A BOCCE BALL

Have a set lying around the house that you haven't touched in years? Bust it out. This is a low-cost way to gain hours of entertainment.

Play as a larger group as intended. Or hone your skills solo so you are ready to be a bocce ball shark at the next summer picnic.

If you're seeking a larger project, consider building a bocce ball court in your backyard. This unique feature may position your home as the destination of choice for future social gatherings.

DATE COMPLETED:

_____

REFLECTIONS:

_____

_____

_____

_____

_____

_____

_____

_____

_____

_____

_____

59. ROLLERSKATE OR ROLLERBLADE

Spruce up your skates or rollerblades and get some exercise around town. If you no longer own a pair of either, head to a roller rink and rent them. Yes, roller rinks still exist! Enjoy the nostalgia in this throwback to your earlier years in addition to the exercise outside of your normal routine.

DATE COMPLETED:

_____

REFLECTIONS:

_____

_____

_____

_____

_____

_____

_____

_____

_____

_____

_____

_____

60. SWIM

Spend time at the pool or beach. You don't need a fancy country club or resort. If you do not already have access to a pool, look to your community's offerings either through public pools, community recreation centers, or the local YMCA.

Alternatively, consider your local lake or creek if those venues permit swimming. Swim for exercise or splash around for fun.

If you are planning a family vacation, prioritize a pool. On a car-camping trip, I found a facility with a lazy river that far exceeded expectations. Countless hours of summertime bliss ensued for everyone.

The objective here as with all these activities is to let go of stress and be present.

DATE COMPLETED:

_____

REFLECTIONS:

_____

_____

_____

_____

_____

_____

_____

_____

_____

_____

_____

61. KAYAK

Kayak, paddle board, or row. Rent a boat or a board on a lake or river nearby. Take in the nature around you. Push yourself until you hit that point where you expect your muscles will feel a good sore the following day.

DATE COMPLETED:

_____

REFLECTIONS:

_____

_____

_____

_____

_____

_____

_____

_____

_____

_____

_____

_____

62. PUTT A ROUND OF MINI GOLF

On a recent summer road trip, playing cheesy carnival-themed indoor golf topped my list of requests. The indoor nature of this tourist-trap offered much-needed relief from the oppressive heat outside. And, the price, to the establishment's credit, reflected the level of quality offered, so ultimately it felt like a bargain. My family had a connective experience both strategizing as a team on each hole and competing individually for the fewest strokes. I came in last place and relished every blacklight, carnival-themed moment we played together.

Hit up that tourist-trap, your usual haunt, or seek the high-end facility you've had your eye on. Support each other in strategy. Keep score or putt for fun. Just remember not to take yourself too seriously. And, remember to appreciate every laughter-filled moment together.

DATE COMPLETED:

_____

REFLECTIONS:

_____

_____

_____

_____

_____

_____

_____

_____

_____

_____

_____

_____

63. JUMP ON A TRAMPOLINE

Trampoline jumping is a low-impact way to relieve stress, improve balance and coordination, and build strength. Plus, it offers a less common way to achieve your cardio workout.

If you have access to a trampoline park, purchase an hour to see how long and high you can jump. Practice that flip if it strikes your fancy. Or double-bounce with a friend for extra adrenaline.

Know the risks and exercise caution, as injuries tend to be more common with this mission than with other adventures, such as croquet or disc golf.

DATE COMPLETED:

_____

REFLECTIONS:

_____

_____

_____

_____

_____

_____

_____

_____

_____

_____

_____

64. RIDE A BIKE

If this is your usual form of exercise, get out there for 20% longer than a usual ride and take on a different route from your normal.

If you haven't ridden your bike in years, clean it off, put air in those tires, and perform whatever other tuning it needs to be safe and functional. If you don't own one, consider renting if your area offers that service. Also consider a free or low-cost used bike online.

Then pick a nice day, grab your helmet, and get out there. Feel the wind on your face and get those leg muscles moving.

Aim to ride for at least 30 minutes.

DATE COMPLETED:

_____

REFLECTIONS:

_____

_____

_____

_____

_____

_____

_____

_____

_____

_____

_____

EXPLORE

Experiencing new things and simply getting outside helps keep us sharp, curious, and appeals to our inner adventurer.

Hiking is one of my personal outlets. Even my wound-up-tight working self could unwind by falling into the rhythm of a moderate day hike, focusing only on putting one foot in front of the other, while the stress of daily work and life melted away. The magic comes from visually taking in new surroundings, but also in reducing stimuli of screens and physically requiring the body to perform beyond the normal laps to and from the water cooler.

Push yourself a little outside of your comfort zone. Get the heart pumping. Explore something new and appreciate letting go of everything that's waiting for you when you return.

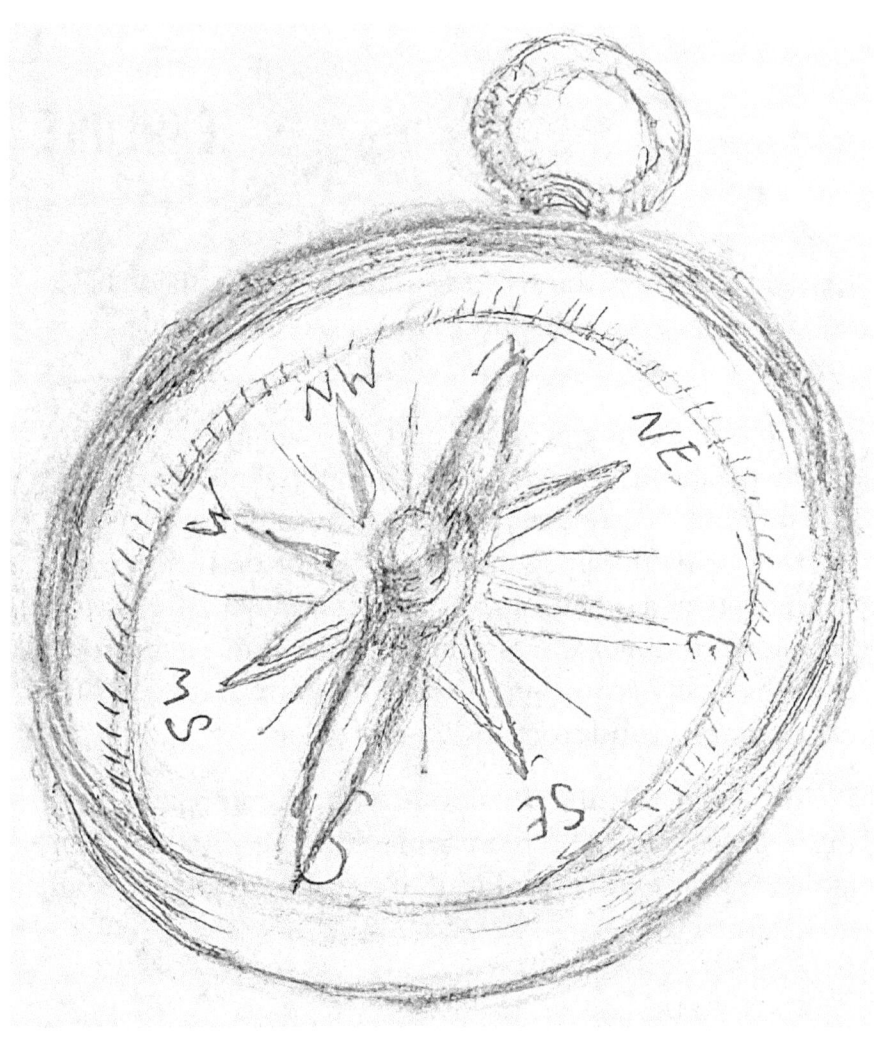

65. TAKE A HIKE!

Search online or your favorite hiking app for a trail new to you. Prepare with the necessary gear for your selection — at a minimum you will want water and sturdy shoes, but you may also benefit from accoutrement including, but not limited to, a compass, map, first aid kit, snacks, sunscreen, and rain gear. Make a day of it.

If possible, keep your phone in your daypack. Some of us rely on digital trail maps, so that's fine. But constant scrolling and searching online is a particular scourge of the unemployed. Be mindful of the mental health benefits you will reap by unplugging from the overstimulation for a few hours.

Remember to leave no trace.

DATE COMPLETED:

_____

HIKE CHOSEN:

_____

_____

NOTES:

_____

_____

_____

_____

_____

_____

_____

_____

_____

_____

66. SLEEP IN THE GREAT OUTDOORS

In a tent, of course! Or open air if that's your preference. Sure, you can hike while camping and camp while hiking. But this mission is specifically focused on sleeping outdoors. Spend at least one overnight in the wilderness.

For the less outdoorsy, backyard and car camping—meaning you can drive directly up to the site—both satisfy this item's requirements. Aim first to locate a campground in your community or an easy getaway from your house. If that's not an option, set up a tent in your backyard or a friend's yard if you live in an urban area.

For those who wish to go all in, commit to backpacking. If you have the time, gear, and ability, aim for a three-day experience. Research shows that the deeper healing benefits of nature kick in at the three-day mark. The relief is so profound, that I've had several people turn to me on day three or four, unprompted and without knowing about the supporting research, to comment on how amazing they feel. If you take others with you, agree together in advance about how often and under what circumstances you will use electronics.

Along my journey, I capitalized on the abundance of time to achieve a major bucket list item: hiking the Inca Trail. This four-day trek in Peru brings hikers up close to less accessible settlements and ruins before ultimately unveiling the divinity of Machu Picchu. Backpacking of this scope is not always financially or logistically feasible. To the extent that it is, however, leverage your time for that mountain or trek that has been on your someday list.

DATE COMPLETED:

_____

VENUE:

_____

_____

REFLECTIONS:

_____

_____

_____

_____

_____

_____

_____

_____

_____

67. WALK A NEW ROUTE

Research shows that getting outside every day for a minimum of ten minutes helps relieve stress and mitigates burnout. Commit to getting outside today even if it's just for a few minutes. While ten minutes is the minimum, thirty or more is ideal. If you regularly walk or run for exercise, seek a new route for today's mission.

Again, leave your cell phone behind for a much-needed break. Pay close attention to what happens around you. Engage all your senses. Listen for the sound of birds chirping. Observe the specific shade of coloring on the fox or deer that wanders past. If you journey along a lake or stream, notice the movement, ripples, or complete stillness in the water. Finally, pause to breath in the honeysuckle that you have always caught a whiff of in your hurried passing.

Give your mind the white space it needs to wander. When you return, take a moment to reflect below on your thoughts, to-do items that emerged, and how you feel overall.

DATE COMPLETED:

_____

REFLECTIONS:

_____

_____

_____

_____

_____

_____

_____

_____

_____

_____

_____

_____

_____

68. SEEK THE PEAK

Identify the highest natural point in your town, county, or state. Make a plan and join the friendly, supportive community of highpointing. The level of technical difficulty and logistics will vary by geographic region, so only attain what is feasible and safe within your abilities and range.

If your county or town highpoint sits on private property, be sure to obtain permission from the landowner before attempting the feat. State highpoints, even those on private land, all offer public access. Some require permits and others only offer entry during certain hours or days of the year. Research your highpoint's accessibility and respect all policies.

As you stand on the highest natural point, pat yourself on the back for the accomplishment of getting there. Whether you drove right up to the U.S. Geological Survey marker or backpacked for several days, you have earned the right to be proud of the journey and adventure that brought you there. At that moment, you will be higher than anyone else in that region, and that's pretty cool. Stand tall, look around, and remind yourself that you can accomplish greatness.

To get you started on your research, here is a list of each state's highest natural point.

Alabama: Cheaha Mountain
Alaska: Denali
Arizona: Humphreys Peak
Arkansas: Magazine Mountain
California: Mt. Whitney
Colorado: Mt. Elbert
Connecticut: Mt. Frissell S. Slope
Delaware: Ebright Azimuth
Florida: Lakewood Park
Georgia: Brasstown Bald
Hawaii: Mauna Kea
Idaho: Mt. Borah
Illinois: Charles Mound
Indiana: Hoosier Hill
Iowa: Hawkeye Point
Kansas: Mount Sunflower
Kentucky: Black Mountain
Louisiana: Driskill Mountain
Maine: Mt. Katahdin
Maryland: Backbone Mountain
Massachusetts: Mount Greylock
Michigan: Mt. Arvon
Minnesota: Eagle Mountain
Mississippi: Woodall Mountain
Missouri: Taum Sauk Mountain
Montana: Granite Peak

Nebraska: Panorama Point
Nevada: Boundary Peak
New Hampshire: Mt. Washington
New Jersey: High Point
New Mexico: Wheeler Peak
New York: Mt. Marcy
North Carolina: Mt. Mitchell
North Dakota: White Butte
Ohio: Campbell Hill
Oklahoma: Black Mesa
Oregon: Mt. Hood
Pennsylvania: Mt. Davis
Rhode Island: Jerimoth Hill
South Carolina: Sassafras Mountain
South Dakota: Black Elk Peak
Tennessee: Clingmans Dome
Texas: Guadalupe Peak
Utah: Kings Peak
Vermont: Mt. Mansfield
Virginia: Mt. Rogers
Washington: Mt. Rainier
Washington DC: Fort Reno
West Virginia: Spruce Knob
Wisconsin: Timms Hill
Wyoming: Gannett Peak

For more information about state highpoints and visitor access, The Highpointers Club and Highpointers Foundation both offer insight and resources to inform your state highpointing adventures ahead. For county highpoints, SummitPost.org is a great resource to kick off your research.

DATE COMPLETED:

_____

TARGET HIGHPOINT(S):

_____

_____

REFLECTIONS AND OBSERVATIONS:

_____

_____

_____

_____

_____

_____

_____

_____

_____

69. TAKE A FUN CLASS

What new hobby or passion do you wish to explore? Curious to learn how to make latte art hearts or leaves? What about a truffle-making workshop?

Enjoy wine, and interested in diving deeper into flavor profiles and growing regions of grapes? Consider a Wine & Spirits Education Trust course either online or in-person. Or, how about going after your motorcycle license?

Whether you wish to learn 3D printing, enhance your sushi-making abilities, or gain proficiency in properly decorating a cake, start by researching the options available in your community or virtually. Set a budget and register for your desired course or workshop.

As budget and time allow, add more into your schedule, but do so one at a time. Wrap up one experience before embarking on the next.

DATE COMPLETED:

REFLECTIONS:

---

70. DEVELOP A SURVIVAL SKILL

Pick a survival or lifesaving skill you have always wanted to learn. Curious about how to make fire without matches? Want the ability to build a shelter in the wild? How about improving your first aid skills or knowing how to signal for help in a variety of locations?

YouTube videos and online courses can guide you. Study up as much as you can for free.

Once you study the how-to mechanics of your new skill, put them to practice. Learning to bandage wounds properly? Grab the gauze and wrap a family member's uninjured arm. Practicing building a fire? Head to your backyard or an open field. Video tutorials alone are not enough to master this skill; it is critical to reinforce the knowledge by doing.

Whichever skill you choose to develop, remember to employ proper safety measures. If you are building fires, be prepared with multiple ways to extinguish the flames — water and soil, for example — before you even attempt the build. Be ready to be successful and safe.

DATE COMPLETED:

_____

SKILL(S):

_____

_____

_____

NOTES:

_____

_____

_____

_____

_____

_____

_____

_____

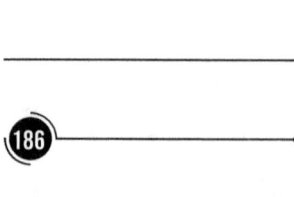

71. UPSKILL

Consider what will help round out your professional knowledge for your next role. Will learning or expanding your understanding of a programming language like Python or R help? Are you lacking a professional certification? Do you require any continuing education (CE) credits? Could you use guidance in building or enhancing a website?

Consider free or low-cost courses online. Coursera is one potential resource that offers both a subscription model and free courses.

If you have been itching to enhance or refine your public speaking skills, look to a local Toastmasters chapter for a safe space with a proven successful structure. To help you find the best fit, start as a visitor in multiple local clubs, as each has its own culture and flow.

After you have achieved your new certification, education, or professional development, remember to tout those new skills on your LinkedIn profile and on your resume.

DATE COMPLETED:

_____

SKILL TARGETED:

_____

_____

_____

REFLECTIONS:

_____

_____

_____

_____

_____

_____

_____

_____

_____

72. LEARN A NEW LANGUAGE

Will learning Mandarin further your career objectives or satisfy a long-standing goal? Go after it with vigor. Traveling to Germany? Get ready for the trip and converse with confidence. Would learning sign language help you personally or professionally? Now is your time. Feel left out when your friends speak ... Klingon? Duolingo can navigate you through that and other languages.

Or maybe you would like to dust off language skills you learned in high school or college. Consider whether you know a native speaker nearby who would be willing to meet up for coffee where you can practice regularly. As a thank you for that person's time, you may want to buy their coffee. Small price for the otherwise free lesson.

To focus on travel-related phrases, check out the library or Audible's offerings.

In addition to the functional terms you will inevitably cover (hello, goodbye, where is the bathroom?), stretch yourself to learn at least one random word that you will likely not need to know. Examples include stapler, vampire, vacuum cleaner, ghost, or fisherman.

Next, challenge yourself to work this word into a conversation in your studied language. I relished the delight and surprise on a Tanzanian's face when I inquired in Swahili, "pilipili hoho?" and received both a genuine smile and an enthusiastic affirmative nod that the food in question was, indeed, green bell pepper.

DATE COMPLETED:

_____

CHOSEN LANGUAGE:

_____

STRETCH WORD & TRANSLATION:

_____

_____

_____

_____

_____

_____

_____

_____

_____

_____

73. VISIT A MUSEUM

The mission today is to explore a museum you haven't yet visited. This doesn't need to be a grand, expensive museum or even a famous one.

Does your town or region offer a free, and perhaps under-visited museum in honor of its history? What about a free museum on cryptography? Or, one related to music? How about one that offers an immersive cooking experience?

For my personal journey, I somehow convinced a long-time friend from high school to join me in standing dumbfounded among 100 square feet of what initially appears to be a rather underwhelming museum in a neighboring town. The entirety of the collection boils down to a dozen photos and a brief chronological recount of the town's history. The timeline is so small, in fact, that it adorns one wall between the visitor's welcome desk and the bathroom with a few stray facts on a perpendicular wall. Had it not been labeled a "museum," we might not have even noticed the content. Despite its lackluster size, we walked away that day with deeper insight into the railroad's influence on the local community, the town's significance in the Civil War, and the progressive initiatives that propelled a community from one of slavery in the 1800s to one focused on educating and supporting African Americans. Explore that kind of place. The overlooked gem in your community.

If the museum normally charges an entrance fee but offers one day or evening of the week for free, plan to attend during the free zone.

Spend several hours soaking in the information, immersive experience, or beauty. Or in a case like mine, read the hundred words on the tiny wall and learn a new historic fact.

DATE COMPLETED:

_____

MUSEUM VISITED:

_____

_____

_____

REFLECTIONS:

_____

_____

_____

_____

_____

_____

_____

_____

_____

74. ATTEND A FREE COMMUNITY EVENT

Search for free or low-cost events in your neighborhood. Look for concerts or other live performances, perhaps at an outdoor venue, film festivals, art exhibitions, holiday-themed events, workshops, outdoor movies, and games.

The goal is to get out of the house, experience something outside of your usual, keep costs low, and perhaps even meet new people.

Summer is an especially great time to seek things like jazz in the park or a weekly outdoor movie screening. In both cases, bring a blanket and some snacks and enjoy the entertainment. Year round, keep your eyes open for various exhibitions, battle of the local bands, and poetry readings. Free events could be right under your nose without you having been aware. Search for the offerings and remember to be present for the experience.

DATE COMPLETED:

_____

COMMUNITY EVENT ATTENDED:

_____

_____

_____

REFLECTIONS:

_____

_____

_____

_____

_____

_____

_____

_____

_____

75. CHANGE YOUR VENUE

You've been sitting at the same desk staring at the same walls while filling out hundreds of job applications. You're getting stale and restless. It's time to move. A location different from your normal venue opens a new world for your mind. New surroundings can lead to heightened creativity, better focus, and higher productivity.

Bring your laptop to a local coffee shop, a park, or a friend's house. Even changing rooms within your home can afford you this benefit. Just do your normal daily outreach and legwork from a different spot.

If this works for you, treat yourself weekly to a venue change. Stay fresh by intentionally varying your location every week for a month.

DATE COMPLETED:

_____

TODAY'S VENUE:

_____

_____

_____

REFLECTIONS:

_____

_____

_____

_____

_____

_____

_____

_____

_____

76. ENFORCE THE LAW

Before you get the wrong idea, this mission does not involve you tapping into your inner John Wick with hand-to-hand combat or artillery. What it does do is offer a front-row seat to those who do enforce the law … in the form of a ride-along.

Many counties offer the opportunity for residents to join an officer for one full or partial shift. This visibility aims to provide the individual with a deeper appreciation for the challenges of an officer's day-to-day accountabilities.

On my 12-hour ride-along experience, I had a front-row seat to traffic stops, noise complaints, a domestic violence call, and even an arrest. Alongside the officer, I accompanied the arrested individual as they appeared before the magistrate at 1 a.m. and got fingerprinted and photographed before ultimately being taken away to a holding cell.

While I can't promise that level of adrenaline and excitement fighting crime in your ride-along, your perspective and appreciation for the heavy lift our law enforcement undertakes on a daily basis may fundamentally change.

For however many hours you are able to join, this will be a solid distraction from life.

Search your county's police department site for the ride-along application form and submit the required details. If you do not see a formal application or instructions online, call your local department to see if this is a service they offer. Your county will likely do a background check to ensure the safety of their officers and, once approved, you will be invited to schedule your timeslot.

Go with an open mind and friendly conversation. Who knows? This may even inspire your next career move.

DATE COMPLETED:

_____

REFLECTIONS:

_____

_____

_____

_____

_____

_____

_____

_____

_____

_____

_____

_____

_____

77. TAKE A LEAP OF FAITH

This adventure is for the particularly curious and open-minded. In this mission, aim to learn about a faith community different from your own.

For those who are religious, I am not suggesting you convert to a new religion. For those who do not identify as religious, I am not advocating for you to become active in any religion.

This mission simply encourages you to be curious about others in your community on a broader level and seek to learn.

Make a list of at least three religions whose tenets differ from your beliefs or upbringing.

Perhaps you would like to learn more about Unitarianism, Hinduism, Buddhism, or the Bahá'í Faith. Search for services near you. Research the requirements and logistics of timing and proper attire. Ensure that services are open and that you will be welcome to attend. Be respectful, open-minded, and friendly. Those communities are welcoming you into an important aspect of their lives. Learn from the experience and reflect.

RELIGIONS TO EXPLORE:

1. _____

2. _____

3. _____

DATE COMPLETED:

_____

REFLECTIONS:

_____

_____

_____

_____

_____

_____

_____

_____

_____

EXPAND YOUR MIND

(PERHAPS EVEN FROM YOUR SOFA)

So far, we have expanded our palate, our cardio, our network, and our drawer space, and we have satisfied our innate need to explore. Here, we focus on challenging our minds to make this experience well-rounded. This section is full of possibilities that can be achieved anywhere, including from the comfort of your sofa. While you may be inclined at times to curl up in a ball and hide under a blanket, leverage that space instead to harness the amazing possibilities inside you.

78. READ A BOOK OR AUDIOBOOK (OR SEVERAL)

Seize the brain space you now have for a book in whichever format you prefer. Order your favorite author's latest book or head to the library for the novel you have been meaning to read for years.

For more inspiration, seek recommendations from close friends who know your style. Or, search *The New York Times* Best Seller list to see if anything strikes your fancy.

Prefer listening while walking, driving, or doing household chores? If you do not have an Audible subscription — or if you have just canceled it from your organizing day — see if your library offers audiobooks to download.

If a book you read years ago still grips you, but you haven't read everything that same author has published, check out as many books as available from the author. Then prioritize the order and commit to reading them.

Use this opportunity to learn something new, work on yourself, or get lost in another world.

DATE COMPLETED:

_____

BOOK(S) CONSUMED:

_____

_____

_____

_____

_____

_____

_____

_____

_____

_____

_____

_____

79. READ AN UPLIFTING ARTICLE

Search for articles that focus on an area of personal growth that you seek to improve. Identify aspects of the article that resonate with you. Formulate a plan to incorporate a piece or all of the advice into your daily routine.

Perhaps you would like to develop pointers on gaining better listening skills or connecting more deeply with others. Maybe your boost comes simply from reading a feel-good piece on rescued animals or good Samaritan efforts. The goal is to read something positive and have a take-away that can help boost your mood or improve your personal skills. The learning should be dinner conversation worthy.

DATE COMPLETED:

_____

SOURCE:

_____

_____

_____

TOPIC:

_____

_____

_____

_____

_____

_____

_____

_____

80. ATTEND AN AUTHOR READING

Keep an eye out for authors coming to town. Attend free book readings and signings when available. Watch for events at your local bookstore or library, or subscribe to a lecture series.

Well-known authors charge a nominal fee for admission. If your favorite author will be reading nearby, splurge for the ticket price. Otherwise, reap the value in discovering a new book and author you have not previously read.

Remember to get your book signed. Use the brief time together to ask the author a thoughtful question or connect in a meaningful way.

Fifteen years prior, my favorite author signed my copy of his latest book, taking careful time to draw a picture of Abraham Lincoln. This felt special and just for me as no one else in line walked away with a masterpiece of Honest Abe. I was too star-struck at the time to inquire about what inspired the drawing, so instead I wondered about it for fifteen years. When I realized the author was returning to town, I seized the opportunity to ask him about the meaning. "Absolutely nothing" came the crushing reply. Despite the realization that it would have been more interesting to leave that question unanswered, this mystery is no longer occupying brain space. Plus, I spent a few hours captively attentive during his reading, not thinking once about the job search. As an added bonus, I now have two more of his books signed with a new story to tell. Certainly time well spent.

DATE COMPLETED:

_____

AUTHOR MET:

_____

_____

REFLECTIONS:

_____

_____

_____

_____

_____

_____

_____

_____

_____

81. ASSEMBLE A JIGSAW PUZZLE

For those who may be skeptical, jigsaw puzzles have far-reaching benefits. They boost problem-solving and short-term memory skills, increase attention to detail, and offer a break from stress and negative thoughts, which, in turn, lowers blood pressure and cortisol levels. This is a long, fancy way of saying jigsaw puzzles are a great stress reliever, perfect for your current state.

Start by considering your baseline enthusiasm for a normal jigsaw puzzle. Now, challenge yourself and step up one size bigger. Would you normally top out at a 500-piece puzzle? Upgrade to 1,000. A pro with the 1,000-piece? Aim for one with 1,500 pieces. If you normally avoid jigsaw puzzles all together, start with a goal of a 500-piece box.

Next, find an image that inspires you or something that represents your fandom. For instance, look to your sports team or a movie series you enjoy. Maybe an animal theme or inspiring cityscape appeals to you.

I started with a cartoon "Where's Waldo"-esque puzzle themed around my favorite NFL football team. Other fun puzzles along my journey include: a mystery puzzle that comes with background reading material and a challenge to solve the crime among an image that does not match the box, vintage license plates from every state forming a map of the county, and a major landmark I visited on a trip.

Have fun with the image you select. No need to torture yourself with, say, a 1,000-piece solid color image. Unless, of course, that has been a long-standing goal of yours. In that case, that's your puzzle. Go after it!

DATE COMPLETED:

_____

PUZZLE CHOSEN:

_____

_____

_____

_____

_____

_____

_____

_____

_____

_____

_____

_____

_____

82. THINK THROUGH A LOGIC PUZZLE

Logic puzzles are a satisfying way to pass time alone or with others. Plus, they exercise your mind, expand creativity, improve thinking skills, and are simply another nice break from the job-search monotony.

Seek out quick logic puzzles online. Good places to start include sites like Puzzle Baron, Puzzlers Paradise, and Brainzilla.

For a longer experience, try something like the Journal 29 "Escape Room" book. Each page is a new puzzle. When you believe you have solved that page's puzzle, enter your answer online. As you solve the puzzle correctly, you receive a new word, called a "key." The puzzles build so the key word to puzzle 29 may be necessary to solve puzzle 32, for instance. Progress through the multiple books at your own pace.

DATE COMPLETED:

_____

PUZZLE CHOSEN:

_____

_____

REFLECTIONS:

_____

_____

_____

_____

_____

_____

_____

_____

_____

_____

83. PLAN YOUR NEXT TRIP

Where have you always wanted to go? What would you like to do there? Sketch out how long you will need for this trip, a full itinerary, and even hotel and transportation options.

Establish a spreadsheet detailing each day, specific activities, time at each event, travel time between sites if applicable, where you will sleep, and estimated cost. Include links in the spreadsheet so you are able to return to your research without re-creating the wheel.

Don't worry about paying for the trip right now, so don't actually book it. Dreaming up the details of the experience is often half the fun and a significant chunk of the work. Without the pressure of paying for it today, dream big and plan for the ideal experience. If you need to, trim and tweak activities later.

Set the plans aside for when you have the financial resources to take the plunge. When you land a new role, you will have already done the challenging part of figuring out logistics for your trip. With a few bookings, all that will be left is for you to go enjoy the fruits of your labor.

DATE COMPLETED:

_____

DESTINATION OF DREAM TRIP:

_____

_____

NEXT STEPS:

_____

_____

_____

_____

_____

_____

_____

_____

_____

_____

84. WRITE A PRODUCT REVIEW

Pick a product or establishment you enjoy and help other potential consumers by posting about your experience with it. While negative aspects of your experience may exist, keep the spirit of today's mission positive, yet candid. If that angle requires you to rethink your review selection, do it.

This can be about anything of which you have firsthand knowledge—a new book, piece of technology, car, museum, tourist attraction, restaurant, or anything that inspires you in a positive way.

Bonus points for helping out a local small business with a well-crafted, genuine, positive review.

DATE COMPLETED:

_____

PRODUCT/ESTABLISHMENT REVIEWED:

_____

_____

_____

_____

_____

_____

_____

_____

_____

_____

_____

_____

_____

85. COMMIT SOMETHING TO MEMORY

Identify a category that you would like to be able to draw knowledge from at a moment's notice. Consider how life might be if you knew each world capital, the Greek alphabet, or all the elements in the periodic table. Perhaps you would like to readily identify someone's astrological sign simply by knowing their birthday. Or maybe rattling off the first 50 decimals to pi holds allure for you.

Pick something that will make you feel impressed with yourself. Then memorize it, and find a way to reinforce the knowledge so it sticks.

Every time I'm descending or climbing a significant number of stairs or when I'm on a steep section of a hike for several hours, I enjoy reciting each U.S. president in order. When that loses its luster, I measure each step by spelling words and phrases using the NATO phonetic alphabet. Both serve to reinforce the knowledge and give my brain a nice distraction from the physical demands in play. Plus, the skill of the NATO alphabet comes in handy when I need to spell something tricky for another person. It's a win all-around.

DATE COMPLETED:

_____

TOPIC DEEP DIVE:

_____

_____

_____

_____

_____

_____

_____

_____

_____

_____

_____

_____

86. LEARN THE RUBIK'S CUBE

Research the necessary steps to solve a Rubik's cube and play with the puzzle until you are successful.

If you already know how to solve a Rubik's cube, challenge yourself to solve it in a shorter time.

DATE COMPLETED:

_____

NOTES:

_____

_____

_____

_____

_____

_____

_____

_____

_____

_____

_____

87. MEDITATE

Meditation, while not for everyone, can be a positive way to reduce stress, increase self-awareness, aid in focusing on the present, unleash creativity, and promote patience.

Look for a targeted meditation related to anxiety, depression, focus, getting to sleep, or being inspired to take on the day. Search on a meditation app or YouTube for what will best support your state and commit. Select the time of day when you will be most receptive to its benefits, whether that is early morning, mid-day, or evening to unwind before bed.

Try lying down during the meditation if that helps.

If you're well-versed at meditation, aim for a 20-minute or longer experience.

DATE COMPLETED:

_____

SOURCE OF MEDITATION:

_____

THEME:

_____

THOUGHTS:

_____

_____

_____

_____

_____

_____

_____

_____

88. TAKE A BREAK FROM SOCIAL MEDIA

Stay off social media for a full waking day. Temporarily hide your apps in a folder on your phone if you need help pausing the habit. If you have an unhealthy relationship with the news or a general proclivity for doom scrolling, add that to today's digital fast as well.

If you don't have any social media accounts and maintain a healthy relationship with news, congrats! Your task is to do a self-scan, identify what drains you mentally, and purge it from the day. Perhaps you spend too much time watching television or are on your computer nonstop. Do you spend countless hours immersed in video games? Take a screen break.

Today is a day off from negative influences, especially if your relationship with it doesn't even register as negative at first. Scan how you feel during the day and how you feel the following day. Combine this avoidant activity with an active one, like hiking or reading a book if needed.

DATE COMPLETED:

_____

REFLECTIONS:

_____

_____

_____

_____

_____

_____

_____

_____

_____

_____

HAVE FUN

No explanation needed.

89. PLAY A NEW (TO YOU) BOARD GAME

Hold a family game night centered around a board game you have never before played. Sure, you've got that set of checkers and game of *Monopoly* in arm's reach. But, recharge the brain with thinking through new rules and strategy that do not automatically come as second nature. Here are some ideas to get the creative juices flowing – *Ticket to Ride*, *Carcassonne*, or my recent new (to me) favorite — *Code Names*.

Alternatively, consider hosting a game night with friends or neighbors. Ask guests to bring a themed drink, snack, or side dish related to the game(s) of the evening. Dress the part for a more complete experience.

Another option is to host a game night murder mystery. Box sets often come with eight personas. Dialogue evolves as each player initiates discussion based on a limited set of knowledge within their pamphlet. Your goal is to identify the murderer among the group. You can build an evening around a full dinner and use the game as a guide with each course. Highly encourage or even require all guests to dress in character for this option.

However simple or elaborate you make this, be sure to let go of stress. Enjoy the journey of playing the game and the company of the people you have invited to join you in this fun.

DATE COMPLETED:

_____

GAME PLAYED:

_____

PLAYERS:

_____

_____

_____

_____

_____

_____

_____

_____

_____

_____

90. PLAY A NEW (TO YOU) CARD GAME

Think bigger than digging out a standard deck of playing cards or your usual game of *Uno*. Always wanted to try *Exploding Kittens*? Heard about *Munchkin*, *Something Wild*, or *Fluxx*? Now is your chance to embark on hours of entertainment.

My personal journey included learning *Taco Cat Goat Cheese Pizza*. My hands may have gotten a little beaten up from the competitive play among the teens teaching me. And, I may have lost by epic proportions — the goal apparently was not to end the game by holding all of the cards. But, man, was it fun to learn from a younger generation and simply be present and connective through active play.

As an alternative twist, teaching others a card game that's new to them and rediscovering the rules for yourself can also qualify. I hadn't played *Hearts* in decades. I knew the rules at one point, but they certainly were not forthcoming beyond the recognition of the game's title. After getting crisp on the online posting of rules, *Hearts* suddenly filled hours of good-natured competitive fun.

SAMPLING LIFE

Learn new rules and a different, complex strategy. Or relearn a game you used to know back in the day. Go all in enjoying the sheer act of being present.

DATE COMPLETED:

_____

GAME PLAYED:

_____

PLAYERS:

_____

_____

_____

_____

_____

_____

_____

_____

_____

_____

91. PLAY HOOKY

When you were working insane hours, what did your ideal day of playing hooky look like? You know, the day you never took, but often fantasized about and frequently wished you could take.

Is it a day at the beach surfing, splashing in the ocean, or tanning? Are you sitting outside at a café, reading a book, and sipping on some amazing beverage? Are you wandering around an art gallery, soaking in all the beauty displayed before you? Window shopping at the mall? Relaxing at a lake waiting for your fishing rod to show signs of resistance?

Whatever your day of hooky was in your vision that you never had time or energy to take, do that today. Hang your "Gone Fishing" sign and go treat yourself, whether it's a day solo or with others. Enjoy the mental release and the self-care that the day brings.

DATE COMPLETED:

_____

HIGHLIGHTS OF THE DAY:

_____

OTHER REFLECTIONS:

_____

_____

_____

_____

_____

_____

_____

_____

_____

_____

_____

92. CELEBRATE AN OBSCURE HOLIDAY

Many of us have at least one holiday that holds importance to us, one where we decorate our home in the name of being festive.

Pick a new or obscure holiday, one that you have not typically celebrated. Maybe National Sailing Day (May 22) where you theme your living room with all-things nautical.

Or consider one that you already enjoy, but that ranks lower on the festivity scale. For example, if you normally put up only one heart for Valentine's Day, ramp it up this year with pinks and reds around the house and on the front door. Add cupids and hearts galore.

Include theme-colored lights, paper decorations, wooden decorations. Keep budget to a minimum by creating a festive look with materials you currently own.

Bonus points if you DIY the decorations.

DATE COMPLETED:

_____

HOLIDAY:

_____

DECORATING IDEAS FOR NEXT YEAR:

_____

_____

_____

_____

_____

_____

_____

_____

_____

_____

_____

93. MAKE A NEW PLAYLIST

Collaborate with others or make your own. Select a theme such as a particular decade, genre, or destination. Gather all songs that appeal to you within that category.

In preparation for a road trip to Georgia, my travel companions and I prepared a playlist of songs that referenced the Peach State. *Midnight Train to Georgia, Chicken Fried, God's Country, Ramblin' Man,* and *The Devil Went Down to Georgia* kicked off an extensive playlist that rolled with us as the miles clicked along.

If a venue doesn't inspire, perhaps curate a list of upbeat songs that you can sing along with while doing the dishes. Design a playlist with a faster tempo for your daily run. If you're heading into a college or high school reunion, revel in the nostalgia with songs from your school-age years.

If appropriate, make your playlist available to others who might have shared the nostalgic experiences with you or enjoy a similar passion.

DATE COMPLETED:

_____

NOTES ABOUT THEMES TO CONSIDER:

_____

SONGS TO INCLUDE:

_____

_____

_____

_____

_____

_____

_____

_____

_____

94. MAKE SOMETHING WITH YOUR HANDS

Creating something physical with your hands promotes cognitive function, boosts mood, increases mindfulness, improves dexterity, and leads to a solid sense of satisfaction with your accomplishment. It can also help mitigate depression and anxiety.

If you don't need any more self-made art in your home, consider creating a piece for a neighbor or a friend. This can be just a surprise friendship gift, or it can serve as a special thank you for anyone who has recently offered you help.

Paint or draw a picture, throw pottery on a wheel, design a clay figure, embroider, knit, or explore woodburning.

These creations can take an hour—a crocheted baby hat or a sketch of the view from your kitchen window, for instance. Or, they may several weeks if you decide to direct a full claymation video or design an intricate piece of furniture.

If your desired project requires more time than today, set a schedule and hold yourself accountable for hitting targets. Ensure that you see the project through to completion.

SAMPLING LIFE

DATE COMPLETED:

_____

CREATION:

_____

REFLECTIONS:

_____

_____

_____

_____

_____

_____

_____

_____

_____

_____

95. DESIGN A DIGITAL CREATION

If you have been itching to build a website or already have a site that could use some work, this is where you will channel your energy. Perhaps, you have an app in mind just waiting to be designed.

Alternatively, create digital art. Do you need a label for the vanilla you made with #11? Whatever your choice, pour your full attention into it.

This creation can take an hour or several weeks. If you require more time than today, set a schedule and hold yourself accountable for hitting targets. Make sure you see this through to completion.

DATE COMPLETED:

_____

DIGITAL CREATION:

_____

SCHEDULE FOR COMPLETION:

_____

_____

_____

_____

_____

_____

_____

_____

_____

_____

96. LEARN THE WORDS TO A SONG

We all have those songs we sing while driving or in the shower. We know most of the words, but not really. Instead, we make up lyrics we either don't remember or have never been able to decipher. Or we stay silent for multiple verses because we have no clue what to sing. And, let's face it: we don't get any better the next time we hear the same song; we continue to sing around the unknown lyrics in the same exact way, repeatedly. Pearl Jam's *Even Flow*, anyone?

If you already know the correct lyrics to every Pearl Jam song, you're particularly well-suited for this mission. You know the drill for researching lyrics, rehearsing, and committing to memory this impressive feat.

Other options to get your creative juices flowing may include one of Taylor Swift's newly released masterpieces. Or, maybe you desire to become fully versed in a faster song from the 1980s like the Bangles' *Walk Like an Egyptian*. How about Macklemore's *Can't Hold Us*? Or Eminem's *Lose Yourself*? Perhaps a song from a Broadway Show — *Guns and Ships* from Hamilton, for instance. (I personally can't sing that fast even when I'm staring at the lyrics!) My bet is that it won't take you long to identify this goal. The song may already be playing in your head as you read this passage.

Now, go ahead, look up those mystery words on the internet and get to work. Once you have committed the lyrics to memory, impress your family and friends with your newly acquired skill. Stay with it until the proper words will stick. This way, you don't backslide a year from now by singing the initial wrong words or employ long swaths of silence for completely unknown lyrics again. Go master it!

DATE COMPLETED:

_____

SONG(S) LEARNED:

_____

_____

_____

_____

_____

_____

_____

_____

_____

_____

97. CONFRONT A FEAR

Where have the clutches of fear held you back? Today we're going to put on our big-kid pants and go after it. Skydiving? Rock climbing? Singing karaoke? Snake handling? Motorcycle license? Public speaking?

If your fear can be addressed with a one-time event, like rock climbing or skydiving, search Groupon or LivingSocial for discount opportunities and book your adventure.

If the thought of being in front of an audience moves your bowels, focus there. Organizations like Toastmasters offer a safe space to hold your hand through the initial process and allow you to live to tell the tale of public speaking. This has an added bonus of upskilling and preparing you for job reentry.

Snakes? Visit a reptile exhibit at the zoo or pet store. Recruit a friend for morale support if needed.

No matter your goal, identify how you intend to stretch yourself, write out a plan including a schedule, and go crush it.

DATE COMPLETED:

_____

FEAR TO OVERCOME:

_____

PLAN TO ACHIEVE GOAL:

_____

_____

_____

_____

_____

_____

_____

_____

_____

98. START A SIDE HUSTLE

Interested in exploring the world of real estate? You have the time to obtain licenses and start building a business.

Do you have a potentially patentable idea? Take first steps, develop a prototype, and begin consulting with an IP attorney to protect your work.

Dream of writing a book? Start sketching the framework and begin writing.

Enjoy designing jewelry? Open an Etsy store or start marketing to your private platform.

What about your long-seeded dream of owning and operating a food truck?

Whatever direction you choose, it will give you a creative outlet and potentially bring in some extra cash that can help bridge the gap during your time of transition. Who knows? You might even keep at it after you land — or transition entirely to this work.

DATE COMPLETED:

_____

SIDE HUSTLE:

_____

NOTES ON NEXT STEPS:

_____

_____

_____

_____

_____

_____

_____

_____

_____

99. GAZE AT THE CLOUDS

As a kid, do you remember laying on the ground and looking up at the clouds? We tend not to restore ourselves in this simple way as adults. Until today.

Cloud gazing can improve your mood, lower stress and anxiety, increase mental health and mindfulness, and spark imagination. With potential benefits like that, get out there.

Grab a blanket, lay down outside, and stare up at the clouds. Identify the shapes you see. Spend a minimum of ten minutes. Set a timer if you need to.

DATE COMPLETED:

_____

CLOUD SHAPES SPOTTED:

_____

_____

_____

_____

_____

_____

_____

_____

_____

_____

100. REFLECT

Journaling, while not an outlet for everyone, is worth a try at least once to see how it goes for you. This form of pointed reflection aids with mental health, enhances communication skills, improves emotional intelligence, inspires creativity, expands self-awareness, and promotes personal growth to name a few benefits.

Now is an important juncture to block off time for this, even if it starts off feeling uncomfortable and unnatural. As you reflect, ensure that you do it without judgment. Be easy on yourself.

If you are inclined, fill pages in a journal. At a minimum, give your brain white space to process through your journey to date.

What is working for you? What's not working? What makes you happy? What triggers you? Do you need additional resources or changes?

Where do you want to be five years from now? Are the actions you are taking today supporting that goal? What needs to stay the same? What needs to change?

DATE COMPLETED:

_____

HIGHLIGHTS OF REFLECTIVE THOUGHTS:

_____

_____

_____

_____

_____

_____

_____

_____

_____

_____

_____

BONUS IDEAS

I just couldn't stop at 100. The ideas kept flowing.

A) Head to a pond, lake, or any other still body of water and skip rocks.

B) Play basketball. Shoot hoops solo or with a group. Make it a competitive game or just for fun—your choice.

C) Build a fort. We turned our sofa upside down and used the entire family room as a playground for our fort. We then popped popcorn and watched a movie. It's a lot of work to put away (give yourself permission to handle that the following day), but so much fun creating.

D) Construct and fly a kite.

E) Rent a paddle boat. Move around for exercise or take a leisurely float around the area.

F) Get lost in a corn maze or other labyrinth.

G) Treat yourself to a magazine. Sign up for a one-year subscription to a magazine you have always wanted to read regularly, but only picked up in the doctor's office. It's a low-cost way to indulge and a forum for your mind to explore new ideas.

H) Make a homemade syrup. Corn syrup and fresh fruit heated on medium heat gets you started on this simple and tasty journey. Try one cup of corn syrup and one cup of fresh raspberries to start the inspiration.

I) Play the trade-up game. We challenged ourselves to start with a small household item (ours was a magnet) and commit to making five trades that day with strangers. This exercise pushed all of us outside of our comfort zone, but resulted in fun conversations, meeting new people, and scoring us a bag of animal crackers and a light up bouncy ball to enjoy together at the end of the day. It's uncomfortable, but also great fun.

FINAL THOUGHTS

My hope is that this resource brings you joy and comfort, and that it serves as a distraction from stress. The stress is real. How we respond to it is up to us.

Remember your current situation is temporary, an intermission of sorts. When you land in a new role, reflect back and appreciate the balance you have created for yourself. Pat yourself on the back for trying something outside of your comfort zone, exploring a new venue, making a new friend, getting organized, and most importantly—celebrating you.

ACKNOWLEDGEMENTS

Gratitude to Sage Ferrari for illustrating the chapter title pages, offering input on the book, and always being up for an adventure.

Admiration to my mom for being a badass motorcycle license holder and a trailblazer for working women. Special thanks to Karen Turay Hartley for humoring me with the museum visit to our neighboring town and for a lifelong friendship of climbing mountains together both literally and figuratively.

Thank you to Meg Marchese for selflessly donating platelets that directly benefit cancer patients in her community and for helping put a spotlight on the blood donation initiative. Thanks to Janna Olson for nudging me as an accountability partner. Brian Erhard, thank you for being a positive force and reminding me of the benefits of playing hooky. Jared Lynn, thank you for inspiring my newfound love of disc golf, teaching me the rules, and getting me set up with initial gear. Disc golf is exactly what I needed to kick off this part of my journey.

Thank you to all of the amazing people I've met on this journey who have kept me positive along the way—

Yogesh Chavda, Mandie Fox, Marek Slodyczka, Julia Sherwin, Amy Steil, and Todd Hoffman to name a few.

Thank you to Three Sisters Farm for sharing their amazingly delicious hot sauce recipe. Chance encounters sometimes yield positive returns and I'm grateful for this one.

Applause to Insights Career Network (ICN) for offering a platform for learning about new employment opportunities, connecting those in transition, and providing content that helps keep people positive during a difficult time. Similarly, hats off to MRxPros for offering engaging content and regular networking opportunities to the insights industry.

Many thanks to those who shared their thoughts and strategies for dealing with long-term unemployment and allowing me to voice them.

Finally, gratitude to Rob Wells for standing by me through this unpredictable journey.

ABOUT THE AUTHOR

 After more than two decades of a professional insights career, Raina Rusnak found herself in a long-term period of unemployment and sought creative ways to stay positive. Raina is the 77th woman on record to have stood on the highest natural point in each state of the continental United States. Raina currently owns her own consulting business. She enjoys logic puzzles, seeking new experiences, and actively learning about the world around her—sampling life. Raina lives in the Washington, DC, area with her daughter and Russian Blue cat.

ABOUT THE ILLUSTRATOR

Sage Ferrari began her art career at the age of five, when she created a piece that did not turn out to her liking. Sage's mom saw potential, framed it, and hung it prominently in the living room, where it hangs to this day. Seeing the strengths of that piece as a constant visual on the wall inspired Sage to keep growing and developing her passion for art.

Sage specializes in illustrating children's books, capturing the personality of pets on canvas, and painting pieces inspired by nature. When not actively sketching or painting, you can find Sage playing the alto sax.